the bedroom book

caroline clifton-mogg

photography by sebastian hedgecoe

the bedroom book

A Bulfinch Press Book

AOL Time Warner Book Group

Boston   New York   London

First published in Great Britain in 2003 by
Mitchell Beazley, an imprint of Octopus
Publishing Group Limited

First United States Edition

ISBN 0-8212-2760-2

Library of Congress Control Number
2002108549

Bulfinch Press is a division of AOL Time
Warner Book Group.

Commissioning Editor Emma Clegg
Executive Art Editor Auberon Hedgecoe
Senior Editor Lara Maiklem
Picture and Location Researcher
Helen Stallion
Designer Geoff Borin
Production Controller Kieran Connelly
Illustrator Carolyn Jenkins
Proofreader Barbara Mellor
Indexer Helen Snaith

The Essentials chapter (pp.142–167) was
structured and written by Melanie Sauzé

Set in Trade Gothic

Printed and bound in China by
Toppan Printing Company Limited

Page 1: a bedroom in a boathouse on the
River Thames; page 2: a classic bed with
woven rattan headboard against a wallpaper
of growing foliage; right: this simple
bedroom combines the contemporary with
the traditional; overleaf: this strong
bedroom is a room of comfort decorated
and furnished in a traditional style.

contents

introduction

In our childhood, the first room that we notice is our own bedroom. Whether it was a shared space or a personal one, the thought of it will have strong associations – the wallpaper, the colours, the surfaces, the fabrics, the decorative features, even the feel of the cupboard handles. These early, vividly remembered experiences colour the strong feelings we later have for subsequent bedrooms, making this private space for many of us the most important room in the house.

previous pages The modern bedroom is an amalgam of many factors: the influence of traditional bed designs; the integration of comforts such as heating and air conditioning; and the introduction of simple decorative ideas, from fitted carpets to well-placed lighting.

left The half-tester was adopted during the Middle Ages, remaining in common use until the nineteenth century. Originally a sign of slightly lower status than the well-upholstered tester, the half-tester's lighter decorative style established its popularity.

right The *Dream of St Ursula*, a painting by Vittore Carpaccio (*c*.1460–1523) shows an early tester bed with a scalloped canopy. There are no curtains: this is probably an authentic depiction of a bed style in the warm humidity of a climate in which palm trees thrive.

Our experience of an early bedroom might be remembered through a mist of nostalgia, but memories of childhood rooms represent an important starting point for the tastes that we later develop. The modern perception of a bedroom is that it should be a personal statement – a haven, a place of calm, and an escape from the trials of the outside world. In addition to this, and the accompanying vagaries of style, most of us will also require the bedroom to be hardworking on a practical level, without losing any of its visual impact. This is quite a demanding goal.

Our contemporary views are, naturally, only the most recent in the historical evolution of bedroom designs and tastes. In the ancient civilizations of Egypt, Greece, and Rome a thousand or so years before the Dark Ages descended over Europe, great care was devoted to the decoration of the bedroom and the role of the bed. In these classical civilizations, beds could be objects of great beauty and were furnished with sheets (often of extremely fine composition), blankets, pillows, and bolsters. The Ancient Egyptians designed ornate and intricate beds, while Greek beds were conceived in the style of a reclining couch. The Romans created many different types of beds for different situations, giving them specific names such as the *lectus genialis*, a bridal bed which stood in the atrium or central court. Roman beds tended to have a framework of bronze, silver, or wood inlaid with ivory or tortoiseshell, resting on gracefully crafted legs or *fulcra*. The mattress would be stuffed with sheep's wool or the down of swans or geese and was supported on the frame with rope webbing or bronze trellis work.

Pliny the Younger, the writer and diarist who lived in AD 61–113, was fascinated by architecture and design, and has given us detailed information about how the Roman ruling classes lived during this period. He wrote

above Canopied beds with intricate wooden carvings were popular during the sixteenth and seventeenth centuries. Where once a fabric canopy would have rested against the wall at the bed's head, wooden headboards were now the fashionable option. In this example at Oxburgh Hall near Peterborough, the half-tester is of intricately carved wood.

right *The Doctor Visits*, a painting by Jan Josef the Elder (1682–1759) depicts a *lit clos* in use. Hidden by curtains during the day, at night the bed was both private and draught-proof.

evocatively of his own bedrooms in his much-loved villa at Laurentum in the foothills of the Apennines. His bedroom suite, built a little distance from the main house, had two bedrooms. The first was "... for use at night which neither the voices of my household, the sea's murmur, nor the noise of a storm can penetrate, any more than the lightning's flash and light of day unless the shutters are open." The second, meanwhile, was "built out to face the sun, and catch its rays the moment it rises, and retains them until after midday ..."

The sophisticated traditions of these early civilizations were lost after the fall of the Roman Empire in AD 476. During the Dark Ages, particularly in Northern Europe, the idea of a separate bedroom was abandoned. The next historical evidence of separate sleeping quarters cannot be traced until the thirteenth century in England – and these were a far cry from the civilized, refined structures of Pliny's time. In the early Middle Ages, feudal life dictated that the lord of the manor should live, eat, and sleep with his household in the great hall of the house, where the fire gave heat and warmth. Privacy was not an option.

As the Middle Ages progressed, what had started as curtained-off alcoves in the great hall developed into separate bedrooms, although these chambers often housed several beds, each one hung with heavy curtains for privacy and warmth. In this period, the design of the bed was rudimentary. Far from being gilded and ornamented, it was little more than a trestle construction with hardly any shape at all. This design then developed into a base of planks and unturned wood, with heavy hangings that were attached to the ceiling above. These ceiling hangings were gradually replaced by testers: canopies that were attached to the actual frame of the bed and supported by four posts. A hanging was draped across the wall at the head of the bed, later to be replaced by a wooden panelled or carved bed head. It is believed that the use of overhead drapes for beds was a response to the fact that sixteenth-century dwellings were often home to animals and insects, and beds with high posts and fabric suspended over the top shielded the occupants from bugs and animal droppings.

Bed hangings developed and became increasingly elaborate until they assumed more importance than the bed itself, which served merely as an armature for the fabrics that were draped over it. Bed curtains were seen as

symbols of wealth and status, and contemporary inventories across Europe itemize, value, and describe the bed hangings in minute detail. The inventory taken after Charles I was executed in 1649 indicated that his bed hangings were of greater value than his Raphael cartoons.

During the sixteenth century, the framework of the bed started to emerge from the enveloping curtain drapes, and bed head and posts were often carved and decorated. Beds were quite considerably larger than they are today. Privacy was still not considered of great consequence and several people would sleep in a single bed at the same time. The Great Bed of Ware, a heavily carved four-poster bed measuring 3.25 m (10 ft 9 in) square, now on display in the Victoria & Albert Museum in London, is mentioned by Shakespeare in *Twelfth Night*. This bed was considered to be large even in its own day.

By this period, the bed was turning into an imposing structure with rich decoration and carving: it was becoming as much of a status symbol as the hangings had previously been, and in certain situations the design of the bed came to reflect the intricacies of the social attitudes of the time. In France under Louis XIV, when court life was far more ritualized and formal than in England, the King's state bed was raised on a dais and came to represent an almost sacred place, the focus of numerous profoundly complex rituals where courtiers congregated and visitors were received. In England, the King's state bedchamber was also a hallowed spot, in this case accessible only to a chosen few. Any state bed, whether royal or not, always assumed a grand appearance, with soaring posts and magnificent hangings. In England and France, many of the nobility followed the sovereign's lead and acquired their own state beds and bedrooms. Such an arrangement was a mark of status, signifying that the family was one of consequence and liable to be receiving visitors of rank. These beds were grand and designed to impress – tall, richly hung, and often crowned with ostrich plumes.

Although the bedroom had increased in size and importance during the late medieval period, it was still viewed as a rich man's room. The humbler homes of the less wealthy would have had purely functional beds, often four-

left A bed in the Oak Room at Wightwick Manor, a National Trust property in the West Midlands built in 1887 and famous for its interior design by William Morris and C E Kempe. The panels behind the bed are painted in the Pre-Raphaelite style of the period and the doors that open outwards also act as a screen. The fabric on the bed is designed by William Morris.

above *Lisbeth with a Yellow Tulip*, by the Scandinavian painter Carl Larssen, did much to popularize the fresh, clean look of painted wood for all household beds, and particularly those for children.

posters, but sometimes just rudimentary structures. If this was not a truckle bed that could be folded away during the day or pushed under other beds, it would probably be masked by a curtain or concealed within a large, draped cupboard. Standard sleeping quarters at that time would have had little other furniture: a table to hold a light, sometimes a set of steps if the bed was high, and the all-important chamber pot.

By the eighteenth century, the bedroom had finally moved upstairs. In seventeenth-century France, the King used to receive morning visitors in his bedchamber, in a ceremony known as the *levée.* Over the next hundred years, this custom was also adopted within the aristocracy. Indeed, until well into the eighteenth century both the English and the French considered it extremely fashionable to receive morning visitors in the bedroom, where the hosts were clad in what was known as a *déshabillé,* an intricate and often ornate informal robe. Etchings and prints of the time show the bedroom full of wig-makers, music teachers, servants, and other friends and acquaintances in early morning communication with the lady of the house. Eighteenth-century bedrooms were used for a number of activities apart from sleeping – including playing games, sewing, writing, and reading. This was where the privacy of the bedroom started to assume real importance.

During the eighteenth century, that unrivalled period of elegance and informed taste, the bedroom became the epitome of fine taste and pure style. Elegant furniture was now an essential component, and new pieces designed for the bedroom included the *pysché,* a full-length mirror hung on a four-legged frame, and the *lavabo,* a tall tripod table fitted with a porcelain basin and jug with legs on castors, which could be moved into an adjoining dressing room or closet during the day.

Early Victorian houses often accommodated surprisingly large numbers of people: in the middle of the nineteenth century, a medium-sized house with four bedrooms and two reception rooms might be home to a married couple, an elderly relative, five children and two live-in servants. So for many early Victorians, rooms used solely as bedrooms were a luxury, although this was to change as the century progressed.

above This bedroom in Burghley House in Stamford, Lincolnshire (built in the latter part of the sixteenth century) contains a version of the traditional *lit clos.* The bed curtain, although of a simple design, is made in a rich fabric and is heavily embellished with *passementerie.*

right Vincent Van Gogh painted this oil-on-canvas picture of his bedroom with a single wooden bed *(Van Gogh's Bedroom at Arles)* in 1888, when he was living in Arles. The bed shape is a classic one, simple and functional.

The look of the average bedroom in a Victorian and Edwardian house was highly furnished: there would be a bed, a wardrobe, a dressing table, chairs, and a washstand. Because the Victorians and Edwardians never saw visitors in their bedrooms, architectural details tended to be simple or streamlined, although in grander houses the guest rooms were often more elaborate in order to reinforce the status of the family. Hygiene was a central consideration for all Victorian households, so all rooms were designed to be easily redecorated, with decorative details, including furniture and fabrics, that were easy to clean. There would be no fitted carpet, but rather a carpet square, mats, or rag rugs; floorboards were usually painted dark brown or stained a dark colour; and wooden beds that were associated with bugs were passed over for the new, hygienic iron bedsteads. Whereas a typical bed of the 1830s was a four-poster in mahogany or beech with heavy curtains, health reforms in the second part of the century hailed the introduction of half-testers of wood, brass, or cast iron, with a decorative canopy and curtains of chintz or cretonne.

Rich colours were favoured until the middle of the century, but by the 1870s lighter colours had become more fashionable and wallpaper, particularly popular with the middle classes, tended to use floral designs, or other unobtrusive, repeated motifs. From the 1860s, beds became plainer, hangings disappeared, and from the 1880s built-in furniture started to appear in the bedroom, with dressing tables, wash stands, and cupboards set into the alcoves either side of a chimney breast, or even built-in seating areas flanking the fireplace.

In the early part of the twentieth century beds seemed to have changed little from those of a hundred years earlier, and it was only in the latter part of the last century that designers started to think creatively about how beds can best complement modern lives. Beds certainly no longer require bed hangings – central heating and air conditioning have made them redundant. Nor do we insist on fashionably prescribed shapes and designs. Instead our bedroom – whether gigantic or minute, just for sleeping or for a miscellany of other activities – can be designed to suit us as individuals. Whether it is to be a work room, an entertainment centre, a gym, or a study, it must be comfortable and it must be attractive.

left *The First Born*, by Frederick William Elwell (1870–1958), is an example of true Victorian sentimentality, but the painting also offers an authentic depiction of a typical late Victorian bedroom. There is a touching rural simplicity to the room setting and to the style of the bed dressing.

above The Larkspur Bedroom at Standen, in West Sussex, is full of typical Victorian artifacts, ranging from the gold-mounted pictures and polished brass bed to the luggage on the floor. The room also has a timeless quality, perhaps because the Victorian style still strongly influences modern tastes. Standen is now owned by the National Trust.

interpreting space

In the planning of any bedroom, the key to success lies in adopting a liberal, lateral approach. There is after all only one constant element, and that is the bed. Beyond this, any existing constraints should be seen as starting points for ideas and innovation. So, rather than imagining a sleeping space as difficult or awkward, think of it instead as an opportunity for creative interpretation.

previous pages This refreshing interpretation of space shows a raised bed structure enclosed in an open box with slatted wooden sides. The bed looks as if it is hovering above the ground, an effect produced by the mirrored panel installed on its base. The theme of parallel horizontal lines recurs throughout the room, in the half-height box structure behind the sofa, and in the venetian blinds at the window.

left This contemporary South African design demonstrates an inspiring use of roof space. Here the bed is set on a high platform close to the stars – or at least to an arched roof of glass bricks.

right Another roof space showing quite a different treatment – beneath this sloping, beamed roof stand a tall bed with a barley-twist wooden headboard, a patchwork quilt, and a rocking chair of woven hickory beside a traditional rag rug.

When an interior designer takes on a new brief, his or her first task is to discover what the occupants require from every room – not just in a practical sense, concerned with how they plan to use the space in question, but also in the abstract, in terms of the atmosphere and experience that they might wish to create. This exercise is particularly important where the bedroom is concerned, for this room is not simply an isolated space in a house or apartment, but rather an integral part of the whole. So take time to consider how the area can be used in the most rational, productive way, and also in a manner that complements, rather than supersedes, the function of other rooms.

In lieu of turning to a designer, or indeed if working in tandem with one, you should first ask yourself some questions about your bedroom. Think about its shape, the available space (which is a different concept), and your requirements thereof – always keeping, as would the designer, a degree of detachment in relation to both questions and answers. Remember that it is your space – perhaps an obvious thought, but one that can often be sidelined in the quest for the perfect room.

Like the dining room, the bedroom was for many years a structured and conventional area, and it is all too easy to accept this formulaic idea of a traditional, standard, inflexible space. But times and thinking have changed. New products, new practices, an increased interest in and access to design influences and inspirations, as well as continuing developments in such essentials as heating and lighting: all these factors mean that the available options are now extremely variable, and the solutions open-ended.

Our modern lifestyles allow a bedroom to be many things – not only a private place and a sleeping zone by definition, but also a space for other activities, such as studying or daytime leisure.

above As a clever combination of imagination and skilfully used space, what could be more charming than a bedroom in a traditional gipsy caravan? Standing in a garden under the trees, the open doors welcome you inside.

right Inside, the caravan has been arranged in an interesting mixture of romance and practicality. Light fabrics and colour maximize the space, and a painted wooden bed and chest of drawers observe the correct scale and provide all the necessities.

what furniture?

As far as bedroom furniture is concerned, we should count it a blessing that we are no longer constrained by the depressing decorative conventions epitomized by the bedroom suite. In the mid-twentieth century, a bedroom would often have contained very specific pieces of furniture: a bed, usually placed centre stage, with matching tables or cupboards on either side; a wardrobe; a chest of drawers; and perhaps a dressing table, all of a kind and all often finished in a dark imposing wood veneer. But today, in the same way that the kitchen has moved on from bland, laminated uniformity, the concept of furnishing the bedroom has moved towards using the pieces that you like and that are appropriate, even though they may not originally have been intended for bedroom use. Consider using furniture such as round or square tables, comfortable chairs, a small sofa, a bookcase perhaps – it is all about what pleases you, rather than about conventional expectations.

small and awkward spaces

A large bedroom that can accommodate all these comfortable pieces may be highly desirable, but the modern reality is that many bedrooms are smaller than you might wish, particularly once that uncompromising article, the bed, has been installed. But a small space is not necessarily a bad space – there are many decorative ways and designer tricks to make the best possible use of the space available, however unconventional it may be. After all, when people sleep in a confined space such as that on offer on a boat, train, or caravan, far from complaining, they positively revel in the novelty.

Some of the most common decorative mistakes are made when planning a small room – any small room, in fact, not just the bedroom. Too often we attempt to miniaturize the room's contents, to scale everything down, in the mistaken belief that small pieces of furniture and accessories will make a little room look larger. Actually, nothing could be further from the truth – while you can always scale up, it is far more difficult to scale down, and when decorating a small space, large, confident pieces work far better than those of dolls' house dimensions.

left Rooms can be draped with fabric to create the impression of a tented enclosure. This, on the other hand, is an extremely comfortable bedroom set inside an actual tent in a Kenyan safari camp.

right Interpreting space means the clever use of what is there: in this cool, underground bedroom the curving stone walls are decorated in such a way as to accentuate the cosy, den-like quality of the room.

far right A traditional wooden-sided bed has been made into a comfort-lover's paradise – strewn with cushions, positioned beside a well-stocked bookshelf, and lit with candles.

overleaf In a small bedroom an understanding of scale and the successful combination of simple elements are essential requirements. Opaque blinds at the window give a sense of space to this tranquil room decorated with authentic oriental discretion.

The bed, for example, is a large piece of furniture, often the largest piece of furniture in the room, and it is unproductive to try and minimize its impact. Instead, in a small room, treat the bed with *élan*. Cover it with a bedspread with a simple or brightly coloured design, and add pieces of furniture of the same scale in order to balance its bulk. The end result will then be one of comfortable warmth rather than of diffident mediocrity. Once again, the bed itself can provide all that you need. New designs often incorporate a headboard that extends into a unit intended to hold lights, books, bottles, and clocks, as well as housing various remote controls. Although these are generally larger than a simple bed, no other furniture will then be needed – and the bed becomes an island of self-sufficiency.

Another effective decorative device for a small room is the constructive use of colour. Do not automatically follow a pale, bland scheme, in the hope that such tones will make the whole space look larger. Instead, follow the same rules used for selecting the furniture – choose bright, strong colours that will inhabit the area with confidence. Similarly, if you are using pattern, a room of restricted size is not the right place to use a small, all-over, or repetitive geometric design, as this will clamour for attention and blind you with its fussiness. The alternative, however, does not have to be an enormous flowing pattern (although that can work well if carried through with confidence): think instead of a medium-size pattern that will add richness and depth, particularly when used as curtains or bed hangings.

A small room must, of course, be well organized – clutter is not, or should not be, permitted. To achieve such an organized space, plan a storage space for everything and install enough shelves, drawers, and cupboards, so that even the untidiest occupants are encouraged to stow everthing away.

Small rooms can often, also through lack of window space, be dark rooms. Strangely, such rooms can be rather successful as bedrooms, as we do after all spend many of the hours of darkness within them. The rationale here is not to attempt to lend them a lightness they do not possess, but rather to emphasize, even exaggerate, the darker side of life – "dark" here meaning cosy, comforting, and warm. Colours, textures, and furniture should all convey the idea of a womb-like space, a nest into which one can crawl. Rules about using colours that reflect rather than absorb light do not apply here. Paint colour should be matt rather than gloss, using warm shades of soft deep pink, ochre yellow, or mole and taupe (those subtle, beige-pink tones beloved of 1950s decorators) to create a sophisticated, welcoming, and all-absorbing effect. The bed itself might have a fur or faux fur throw or spread, the floor would be carpeted and the lighting subtle and often concealed.

Small bedrooms that are complete in themselves are one thing; small bed spaces fitted into awkward areas are quite another. Because of space restrictions, beds are often fitted into the most unprepossessing and cramped corners – under the stairs perhaps, or set inside a disused cupboard, or positioned under the eaves in an attic. The key consideration is to make the most of any architectural feature, no matter how initially difficult it may seem – and this would include a sloping ceiling, exterior stone walls, and any other challenging elements of an interior. An awkward, strangely angled space can always be made interesting by using colour in a dramatic way, or through the use of textiles as curtains, drapes, or hangings. Traditionally, particularly in Europe, pattern is used to disguise awkward shapes – a room under the eaves, for example, might have every surface covered in one design, thereby camouflaging sharp or irregular angles.

far left The use of spatial divisions to provide separate working and sleeping areas can really maximize the available space. Here, each carefully chosen element, from the angled lamp to the metal ladder, is an integral part of the overall composition.

left A clever update on traditional bunk beds, these two simply dressed platform beds are enclosed within deep bases. Texture and colour have been used to make a harmonious whole.

right This most awkward of spaces – boasting sloping eaves, a tiny window, a protruding chimney breast and a vertical supporting beam – required an ingenious approach. With a plain, decorative scheme and a few simple furnishings, the comfortable bed and the natural light from the window beyond the chimney breast form a tempting prospect.

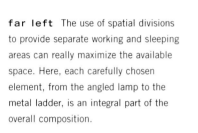

right Lateral thinking can produce the most inventive of solutions. Here the bed has a hinged screen designed around it, which can either be drawn around the bed for privacy, or pulled back to form a partition across the room.

above left Folding beds do not have to look dull or run of the mill. This bed folds down from a cleverly designed space that incorporates both storage and a night table with reading light.

left Another fold-up bed design solution making imaginative use of a confined space. The bed retracts into the wall, and the look is both light and contemporary.

above This modern take on the *lit clos* is a built-in design, literally a bed in a box. It has everything you could possibly need surrounding it, including storage spaces ranged above and below.

platforms and mezzanines

These structural features are often considered only as part of the larger bedroom space, and yet they can also be extremely useful in a conventional small room with high ceilings. It seems obvious in theory, but not everyone thinks in terms of designing upwards – yet a well-designed bed platform instantly adds new space within the room that would otherwise be wasted. Like a super-sophisticated bunk, a bed platform allows the space beneath to be designed as storage, a work area, or a comfortable sitting space.

enclosed beds

Paradoxically, enclosing a bed can add a sense of space, and although this is hardly a new idea, it none the less remains an invaluable one. From medieval times, the enclosed bed (or *lit clos*) was found in simple houses across Europe: extremely practical, it was built against a wall or within an alcove, sometimes with cupboards around it. Thus enclosed on three sides, the bed alcove was rendered entirely private during the day by means of a curtain or sometimes a pair of shutters. Like many old ideas, this one still has numerous applications in the modern world – a built-in bed can be closed off, with or without the addition of storage space to either side or above and below, and placed either in its own room or within a larger living area.

The ultimate built-in bed must be one that is invisible. Beds that are made as one unit and seen only when needed have developed in sophistication since the first days of the rolling truckle or folding camp bed that could be shoved into a cupboard. The wall-hung bed has benefited greatly from modern technology, and today such beds can be found in many guises – from the basic bed that simply pulls down, to the bed which comes as part of a modular, decorative storage unit. Although such units are rarely the *dernier cri* in design terms, the base surface that is visible to the room can usually be well disguised – painted, decorated, hung with pictures, or otherwise treated in a manner that unites it with the rest of the room.

left This dramatic modern space is set within a rural landscape of trees and light. There are concealed sliding doors throughout the space: in this view run between the bedroom and the main living area. This structural device means that the owners can choose to have a seamless, open-plan space (as illustrated), or one with enclosed, private havens.

above A detail of the same location, showing the view from the bedroom area on the ground floor. The spiral staircase rises behind the door shown to the left of the picture, while to the right is a view of the bathroom – which could be hidden behind another sliding door.

the working bedroom

Solutions such as hiding the bed come to the fore when the bedroom is also to be used as a work or study space – as is increasingly often the case today. If you intend to utilize your bedroom for work as well as for leisure, it is important to note precisely the uses you intend to make of it, and the equipment and tools you will want to keep there. Will the secondary life of your bedroom be practical – for activities such as ironing, dressmaking or sewing? Or will it be a place for office work, involving files, papers, computers, and other technical equipment? Whatever its secondary use (and remember, it *is* secondary), do not forget that it must be possible easily to hide from sleeping view the physical remnants of the day's work. It is not helpful to see around you, last thing at night and first thing in the morning, invasive reminders of a less relaxing life, so work out a comprehensive storage scheme before you start

planning – whether you choose a highly organized, made-to-measure variety or the more improvised option of a floor-length cloth draped over a table.

This, of course, is another area in which the mezzanine, raised platform, or gallery can come into its own. Constructed to hold the bed in spacious comfort, a mezzanine platform provides an area beneath it in which another domestic life – of whatever description – can take place. The whole space can, and probably should, be decorated in a way that clearly defines the difference between the activities of night and day.

children's rooms

The most important goal where children's rooms are concerned is to try to achieve a reasonable compromise between your respective needs – in terms both of style, and of balancing practicality and fun, because a child's bedroom

far left Imposing a domestic structure on an industrial space requires strong interior design solutions. Here, the sleeping platform suspended over the dining area has been constructed in a quasi-industrial manner, in keeping with the surrounding architecture.

left Simple and classic in style, a sleeping platform above a cooking area has been designed with a simple wooden balustrade. Wood has been used predominantly throughout, lending a coherent look to the whole.

right Platform sleeping areas can be incorporated into completely traditional surroundings. The balcony bedroom in this Spanish location uses a rough, stained wood for the steps and balustrade, linking them with the old wood of the ceiling.

should certainly be fun. Both girls and boys can be highly specific in their bedroom wish list, very often down to the exact shade of the walls, although girls tend to be more vociferous in their suggestions. The colour debate is tricky – their choice is often precisely what you would not have chosen, for adult tastes rarely coincide with those of children and subtle tastes tend to develop later in life. The decoration of his or her own room is a serious matter for a child. The perspective of youth makes everything far clearer and this applies equally to colour preferences – bright pink is better than blush, sunshine yellow preferable to primrose. This may be one of the first opportunities for a child to assert his or her independence, and I do feel that if they really, really want an all-black room, say, then only they will truly suffer and the results will certainly teach them an early lesson both in decoration and in the consequences of choice.

It is important for the adult to remember that young children change in their tastes and maturity faster than the decoration around them – what may thrill this year may be completely wrong in twelve months' time. So simple is better than complicated, and moderate investment, as far as the decoration is concerned, is wiser than monetary overkill.

far left When two beds are to be contained within the same room, symmetry and order are required. In this shared bedroom everything is twinned, down to the matching dolls' houses at the end of each bed.

left A young girl's bedroom that is small in size has been made to look like the inside of a painted box, with a wooden bed hung with simple curtains and a painted ribbon motif repeated on the bed and walls.

above The ultimate in cool and a clever balancing act between privacy and integration, this warehouse space has a teenager's sleeping area constructed in a free-standing module with every appropriate convenience at hand.

Where a certain investment can usefully be considered is in the choice and arrangement of the permanent furnishings of a child's room. However small the room, allow for as much floor space as possible – this is vital for games, reading, the construction of edifices, and general reclining. A table that doubles as a desk is always a good addition, and is a form of storage that allows a fairly rapid transition from chaos to order. Other than this, the bed should be strong – it will probably be used as a camp, trampoline, bus, or plane. It should also, most importantly, be furnished with a good reading light to encourage reading in a relaxed atmosphere. Blinds or curtains should be light-proof, and attached securely to the walls; the walls should be decorated in a washable finish, as those wide, blank expanses can often prove irresistible; and the floors should be covered, if at all, with washable rugs. If you get it right, your child may remember this first bedroom all their life with pleasure and nostalgia – and what could be more rewarding than that?

combined bedroom and bathroom

Not so long ago there was only a single bathroom within each home (and for some even this was an inaccessible luxury). The bathroom was communal and a distant, chilling trek from any bedroom. One of the most significant changes in domestic life is the emergence of the dedicated bathroom as a desirable, if not essential, addition to the bedroom. Not only that, but where once a bathroom or bathing area leading directly off the bedroom was considered the ultimate in luxury, now it is almost a standard element in many houses of any pretension – at least as far as the principal bedroom is concerned.

There is no reason why the bath has to be behind closed doors – this is just a hangover from the conversion of a separate room into an *en suite* bathroom. If the combined area is large enough (too small is not good, bringing as it does the attendant problems of steam and damp towels) it can be in the bedroom itself, and in many cases this is just a question of removing an internal wall. The advantage is an added sense of space, as well as a certain air of vintage Hollywood glamour, while modern developments in ventilation and heating make it a feasible alternative. Most of us would prefer the lavatory

above Skywood House, designed by Foster and Partners, is a dramatic interpretation of a highly modern space. Bed and bath have equal emphasis, with the bath distanced from the bed by a wall unit that also acts as storage.

right Water is the central feature of Skywood House. Because the vast expanse of glass windows overlooks it, the water becomes an intrinsic part of the room.

overleaf In contrast to the shimmer of water beyond the bed, the other side of the room, beyond the bath, frames another elemental scene, but this time one of trees, grass, and sky.

to be in a separate enclosure, but perhaps surprisingly this is simply a matter of choice, there being no hygiene regulations to prevent an open-plan installation. The overall effect of such an all-in-one sleeping and bathing area becomes even grander when it looks out over a private space – such as a balcony, roof terrace, or garden.

open-plan areas

For a number of reasons, many people today are choosing to live in one large space. This is largely because they no longer desire a home delineated by the conventional boundaries of walls, doors, and other traditional architectural devices. If you yearn for an open-plan space, then define early on exactly what you hope to gain from the living space – apart, that is, from space itself. Any space, whether large or small, needs to be defined in order to clarify exactly what will happen where: there must, for example, be a food preparation space, a living/working space, and a sleeping/bathing space.

The sleeping/bathing space needs careful consideration, for living in a large, modern space offers in some senses both the best and the worst of

above Interpreting space can involve moving away from conventional geometric shapes and orthodox structures. Here, a curved wall keeps the bathing area cleverly hidden from the bedroom while still embracing it within the same space.

right A simple and striking combined bedroom and bathroom, in which you could almost literally fall out of bed and into the bath. Raised on a dais, the latter is surrounded by a half-height storage unit.

far right In this simple, clean-lined bedroom, the bathroom is brought into the bedroom visually through glass-panelled double doors. These give an element of privacy, while at the same time letting maximum light into the bedroom.

bedroom worlds – enough space to arrange the bed in some style, and yet often too much space to offer the essential privacy that you desire. Despite the protestations of early minimalists, few people feel comfortable sleeping in a bed that is simply stranded in the middle of a vast floor: boundaries are essential, no matter how lightly drawn.

In this context, for "open space" read "open mind": modern materials and construction methods mean that now almost any architectural or design solution is feasible. Simplest of all, the sleeping area might be enclosed by paper, wood, or glass screens that fold or slide; it may be hidden behind wooden, slatted blinds; it might sit behind doors that can be concealed within a reveal; or it could be raised onto a platform and therefore be unseen from below. Indeed, if the total living space is large, different levels are sometimes a design essential, and one or several mezzanine areas can break up the area both naturally and in a way that defines both the space and its limits.

A sleeping space might be designed behind a partial wall – one that does not reach full height or width, made of plaster perhaps, or light-diffusing, opaque glass. It can be a half wall, a curved wall, a wall pierced with light-giving spaces, it can wrap around to enclose, or surge forward to connect with other areas. It can be as low as a garden wall, or as high as the ceiling.

The bed might be designed as part of a purpose-made unit in which one side holds books and decorative objects, while the other is a luxurious sleeping console that houses the bed itself, alongside built-in remote-control panels, lighting, and storage facilities. The bed could even appear under the different guise of a seating area during the day, and the whole sleeping space might lead to a private roof space, a garden, or a courtyard.

All these suggestions serve to emphasize that there is no limit to the ways in which a bed area can be integrated constructively into a far larger space. At the risk of stating the obvious, it is always helpful to leaf through design and architectural magazines and books – not necessarily in order to regurgitate any of the ideas wholesale, but rather to see practical examples of what can and has been done, and to reinterpret these concepts so that they work in your particular space and fit your particular needs.

left In the Crescent House, designed by Foster and Partners, simplicity is key. The sophisticated effect of creating a source of natural light at the head of the bed sets a serene mood, as does the elimination of any detail that might detract from the essential quality of a room for sleeping.

above The defining crescent shape of this house means that the walls respond in kind, curving and creating organic barriers between the bedroom and other parts of the house.

There are occasions when, as an alternative to an existing internal space, a separate structure outside the central building can be used as a bedroom: a garden studio, or an old wooden caravan, or even a redundant railway carriage, like the old Pullman coach shown here. If you have such a place suitable for sleeping, then do your utmost to retain a sense of the charm and originality of the setting in its decoration and design. To make the most of the element of novelty, rather than emphasizing the potential drawbacks of any space limitations, try to make the interiors of these structures as comfortable as possible, and as fitting to their purpose (in this case sleeping) as they can be. Since noone is going to commend the Pullman coach room for its spaciousness and height, exaggerate its contrasting qualities. Make the most of the miniature, and design the bedroom as a cosy, comfortable, snug hideaway for the visitor. The most essential factor in limited spaces such as these is to give considered thought to the immediate, practical needs of the sleeper, and to ensure that all the associated, back-up elements – such as lighting, warmth, and ventilation – are easy to reach, simple to operate, and arranged close to hand.

above Slumbering on a train is one of the ultimate sleeping experiences – and, in truth one that is even better when the train is stationary. What could be more inviting than the view through the window into this softly lit Pullman carriage?

right In such a confined space, the tall, polished wooden beds – the gloss of which contrasts pleasurably with the crisp white bed linen – give a confident air of luxury and comfort.

far right Sleeping on a boat is another experience that has romantic appeal, and this houseboat on the River Thames creates a pleasantly soothing atmosphere. This shipshape bedroom combines the best of both nautical and terrestial worlds.

room styles

Style is a highly personal affair – an individual expression of preference, experience, and lifestyle. Although many successful rooms are created by mixing periods, styles, and colours, it is a good idea to have both a starting and a finishing point – and to ensure that beyond its visual style, the bedroom is pleasant, harmonious, and above all comfortable to spend time in.

previous pages A bedroom should revolve around style and this room does just that: fittingly located in Venice, it boasts a monumental bed with furniture and furnishings to match.

left Every decorative style can be interpreted in many different ways, and none more so than the traditional. This dramatic bedroom belonging to London-based designer David Hare is orientated around the neo-classical style, and uses colour to give it a dramatic twist.

right Another, very different, example of a bedroom designed in a traditional style. The lightness and freshness of this room is emphasized by the cool, neutral colour palette, the polished wooden floor, and the large, unadorned windows.

Giving a bedroom your own style signature is as essential as buying the most comfortable bed available. Do you want the bedroom to be decoratively in tune with the rest of the house, or would you prefer it to be in complete contrast? It depends on how much of a statement you want the bedroom to make and how much you want to emphasize the fact that this is personal and private, rather than public, territory. Generally, I would advise retaining a decorative link, however slight, in terms of either colour or style.

Just as every house or apartment has a personality of its own – that impression as you walk through the front door – so too do rooms. The personality of a bedroom is not always obviously defined, and this is where you need to extract the mood of your room and decorate it accordingly. Some rooms emanate an air of serenity, while others feel lively and vivacious. The most successful decoration builds sensitively around these interior atmospheres.

In many cases a completely new decorative scheme is neither feasible nor desirable. If you do not want to change everything, but merely to create a fresh, updated look, then simply use colour and textiles: the most important elements in any scheme, these can dramatically alter a room's atmosphere.

When thinking about the particulars of style, do try to avoid what might be termed "Disneyland design": just because you so enjoyed the vibrant colour and textures of Morocco on holiday, for instance, doesn't mean that your bedroom should look like a cut-and-paste kit of a room in a *souk*. Interior decoration is like fashion. Just as we are told that the most successful way of dressing is to combine different pieces in order to arrive at a coherent look – some of them old, some of them new, a simple outfit anchored with striking accessories, everything combining into a stylish and flattering ensemble – so it is with decoration: edit, adapt, borrow, and succeed.

Colour is perhaps more important in the bedroom than in any other room: one late or sleepless night and your view of the next day will be hugely influenced by the colour and tones around you when you wake the next morning. On the walls, liverish or bilious colours such as some shades of green can be difficult, as can very bright, fluorescent shades. The bedroom is often the room where a favourite colour is used with relative abandon, but do exercise caution as it really is easy to use a colour to excess. By all means choose a favourite colour, but perhaps use a softer tone than you would normally. It is remarkably easy to overdo it – this is an instance where Mies van der Rohe's famous design phrase "less is more" can be put into practical effect.

Pattern is a double-edged sword in the same way as colour. On the one hand, the bedroom seems just the place to use all those fabrics that you have long coveted. But again, tread with caution. One pattern used everywhere, particularly if you are thinking of dressing the bed, is just too much. And if you use more than one pattern, life becomes even more difficult. Too many contrasting textiles and fighting fabrics and papers will give you feelings of disorder and anxiety. Question your choices and pin up samples on the wall for a while. This is not to say that you can't integrate all the elements you are planning – but remember the twin values of balance and scale, which should be integral to whatever style you select.

above Charles Rennie Mackintosh, born in 1868, was a designer working in a style that was before his time, shown by this design for a bedroom. Using a clean and angular style, with much useof reflective surfaces, his work was influential throughout a large part of the twentieth century.

right A traditional design from Northern Europe, this Gustavian-style bedroom contains many timeless elements: the stripped floor, the canopied wooden bed, and the comfortable wooden chairs are all just as appealing today as they were two hundred years ago.

traditional styles

Historically, the bedroom has always been a place where much effort has been expended and considerable sums invested: lavishly worked bed hangings in tapestry and embroidery were often the most valuable items listed in household inventories, and we can still appreciate the wonderful embroidered and decorated hangings that were displayed prominently in many a stately home.

For certain people today, a bedroom should still reflect those opulent aspects of the traditional period bedroom. Yet few people opt for a pastiche or replica, with all their attendant disadvantages: rather they look for a design that embraces the most attractive aspects of period design and decoration, bringing out all the comfort, warmth, texture, and colour that this implies.

Your first decision should be whether you are going to use any antique furniture, or whether you would prefer to convey an impression of, say, the seventeenth, eighteenth, or nineteenth centuries. If you are lucky enough to own any pieces of period furniture, in particular a period bed, then it would obviously be a smart move to use this, giving it a starring role and building the room around it. If antiques are not your style, however, you might prefer to emulate the period look with a reproduction bed. Alternatively, you may prefer simply to suggest the period, using instantly recognizable colour or patterns to suggest a particular era.

Certain periods were stylistically more refined than others and these are the periods to which we are drawn instinctively today. Think of the styles of the eighteenth and early nineteenth centuries, from Georgian and Gustavian to Empire and Regency, when rooms in both Europe and America (and particularly bedrooms) were decorated in a light and graceful manner, with inventiveness and charm. The posts of frame beds were less substantial than they had been in the sixteenth and early seventeenth centuries: as the hangings now encompassed the bed frame, there was no longer the need to give the frame itself such significance. This is good news for anyone seeking to emulate this period in design terms, because the emphasis can be laid on the hangings, rather than on the bed itself.

Beds of this historical period featured canopies that were either raised or attached to the wall. This time also saw the appearance of designs such as the bedchamber of the famous Madame Récamier, the celebrated French style-setter of the late eighteenth and early nineteenth centuries, whose bed hangings consisted of fringed white Indian muslin spangled with gold stars. Materials then used included silks, taffetas, damasks, mohair, and the new, hugely fashionable, painted and flowered chintzes imported from India. If the idea of such airy, romantic charm appeals, then choose one of the document prints taken from these early designs now reproduced on linen, cotton, or silk. Alternatively, use a sheer, see-through fabric in copious quantities.

Easier to source might be a Victorian style, but rather than the aspidistra-strewn, overblown, heavy wooden look of the Great Exhibition years, consider

left Another Gustavian style from Scandinavia, this time featuring a bed with hangings similar to those of a traditional *lit clos*. The room is simply furnished, so emphasizing the gleaming gilding on picture frames and furniture.

above Until the eighteenth century, it was traditional for wooden beds of any standing to be heavily carved. In this room with wooden beams and door, the bed is placed in front of heavy curtains that frame both the window and the bed.

above left The four-poster or tester bed has appeared in many guises over the centuries. Here, a pair of English eighteenth-century four-poster beds have been dressed with Moorish-style canopies that echo the decoration on the wall.

above right This London bedroom is designed in traditional grand eighteenth-century style. The full tester bed is dressed with intricately made curtains and a canopy, and the bedcover is quilted in the same material that is used to cover the walls.

right A finely carved four-poster bed such as this example requires no curtains, as they would only detract from its charm. The carving and skilfully turned posts demand our full attention, while the rest of the room is of secondary importance.

left A successful strategy when faced with a four-poster bed of some substance can be to dress the bed with the simplest of curtains in restrained colours – in this case cool shades of cream and white.

overleaf This bedroom in interior decorator Christophe Gollut's Canary Islands home is the epitome of rural charm. Old Portuguese metal bedsteads are covered with textiles from Jaipur, while the fringed tablecloth is Moroccan.

using an iron bed. Despite being a novelty, these were much loved by forward-looking Victorians, as they were deemed to be more hygienic than the huge wooden alternatives. Once acquired, an iron bed could be painted or left in its original state. These airy, highly feminine beds look charming against a wall painted in a soft, chalky colour, or papered in a small flower-strewn design.

The early part of the twentieth century also has its charms as a decorative period. It is quite possible to decorate a room in either sinuous Art Nouveau or the very different, angular, and geometric Arts and Crafts style, and reproductions of the wallpapers and fabrics of those years are available in abundance. The designs of this period are still underrated, but are fascinating to study as they reveal the early development of contemporary design.

country styles

Also traditional, although not in a period sense, is the perennial appeal of the countryside – this is not so much a style as a way of thinking, and it can be conjured up as easily in the centre of a town as in a country village. Country style does not have to be expensive to achieve – indeed, many would say that

far left All the furniture here, including the tall, posted beds made of tiger maple, is reminiscent of the functional style introduced by the Shakers in nineteenth-century America.

left The bedding of this traditional American country bed, known as a cannonball bed, rests on ropes that can be tightened by turning pegs within the structure. A fine patchwork quilt and a tapered-leg side table complete the nostalgic picture.

above A mixture of different country influences from across the American continent, this bedroom in a converted New England barn combines North American rugs with a carved wooden cupboard from Mexico.

it works best when deliberately inexpensive elements are used, particularly where textiles are concerned. This style is the choice for those who prefer an Aga stove to high-tech cookers, who like blankets and crisp sheets instead of a duvet, and who use wicker baskets instead of plastic shoppers. It is a style that evokes dappled sunlight filtering through the boughs of old fruit trees, geraniums spilling out of mossy pots, humming bumble bees, and pirouetting butterflies. Country style has had its up and downs over the years, reviled and then applauded, but for many it will never go out of fashion, for it is a way of life.

The constants in a country style are a feeling of air, a sense of space, and a lightness of touch. No matter how urban we may be, many of us have a whiff of the country in our soul, and the bedroom is perhaps the best place to unleash this inclination.

Country style does not mean heavy drapes and swags at the window, but rather light curtains with simple headings. It can be particularly successful in a small room, or in a room under the eaves with tiny windows framed by curtains caught back with ribbon or rope. A room with larger windows should still be treated with a light touch, and in a simple manner – no swags and tails

above Floral designs should always be chosen with great care. Although this combination features three different sets of florals on the linen, the bed and the curtains, they coordinate well, because each design is on a white background.

right An all-over pattern, such as this wallpaper design, needs strong, simple pieces of furniture, which will complement it and integrate the design into the overall scheme. This is a detail of the bedroom shown on the far right.

far right This bedroom has to be in the country, filled as it is with natural images of flowers and butterflies. The curtains have been hung simply so that the natural landscape beyond the window also becomes a feature of the room.

left A high window has been drawn cleverly into the decorative scheme of this Swiss bedroom by the wall hanging, which falls down from the window behind the beds. Curtains are not needed, as shutters suit the simple look.

right A clever juxtaposition of vertical and diagonal elements claims our attention in this bedroom beneath the eaves. The bars of the iron bed, painted black, draw the eye up towards the beamed roof.

far right Certain materials and artifacts are associated with a rural environment. Here, the combination of wicker and cane, a rag rug, and a traditional patchwork quilt all strongly suggest the country.

and no heavy, lined pelmets. A pole with the curtain hung on rings is always effective, but take care to ensure that the proportions of the pole are correct. The wider and taller the window, the thicker the pole can be (a small window should have a correspondingly narrower pole). And if the pole is wooden, consider the colour or stain with the colour and pattern of the curtain material. If the poles are metal, then beware of buying brass that is too shiny, as this can look cheap. You can buy antique and reproduction metal rails that are ridged and channelled. Think also about the finials and the brackets – a plain white pole can look wonderful when held in place by two or three ornate antique brackets. The finials should always be in proportion to the thickness of the pole as well as to the height of the window.

Country colours are soft and soothing: pale blues, greens, yellows, pinks, lilacs, and creams, that give the impression of being bleached by the sun.

Layers of colour, built up and rubbed back, can achieve the softness of touch that is required. The country floor could be plain, untreated wooden boards or pale terracotta tiles or bricks (the latter can be treated to reduce the dust). A rug could be introduced next to the bed: either a traditional, multi-coloured rag rug, or one made from seagrass or sisal, both textures that suit the country look. If the condition of the floor is so poor that it is necessary to carpet it, choose a flat-weave carpet rather one with a pile, and opt for a neutral colour that will complement the natural elements in the rest of the space.

As far as pattern goes, the country bedroom is not the place for clever abstracts and large-scale patterns. Every motif should be immediately recognizable – a dot, a square, a stripe, a flower. Some traditional designs such as the Indian tree pattern work well, and a faded chintz is the indisputed queen of country style, which can always be included with great success.

An antique quilt in appliqué, patchwork, or stitching would be an ideal accessory for a country bedroom. The scraps of fabric used in these old quilts were often created with vegetable dyes, which fade elegantly over time to create bleached, country-style colour palettes. Such a quilt does not have to be as large as your bed, as it can be used on top of a plain cover. Almost any antique textile can be incorporated into a country bedroom – except perhaps the grandest damasks and brocades. Not only can whole lengths be used as curtains, but smaller remnants can be used to cover a stool or cushion. Assorted Paisley shawls, whether old or new, perfect or flawed, can work as warm and subtle bed curtains as well as a bed cover: they do not have to match, but merely share the same colour values.

The country bed may be made of wood or metal, but it could equally be a simple divan. It will probably have several plump pillows – enough to make having breakfast in bed the pleasure that it should always be. Behind the bed there might be a wooden headboard, carved, stripped, or painted. It might also be of brass or iron, or it might be covered with fabric. It would not, however, be padded or buttoned, and it would not be finished with new velvet or brocade, but with a simpler design such as checked gingham (the quintessential country design), or again with a piece of something old: an embroidered panel, part of an old patchwork quilt, or even a loose slip-cover made from a piece of old, starched linen and fastened with ties.

Country style is always romantic, and this seductive combination of flowers, soft fabrics, and quiet colours and textures means that a country bedroom is recognizable anywhere in the world – with the odd stylistic difference. An English country style might have pale, icecream colour walls above polished wooden boards and faded curtains in a small or floral design. In France, the rough plaster walls might be in the colour of the Provençal countryside – with sunshine, sky, and lavender fields evoked by familiar fabrics with small repeated patterns based on stylized plant forms. In the USA, country style might be pioneer style – a patchwork quilt on a wooden bed, rag rugs on the floor, and stencilled floors and walls. The design and decoration used by the American Shaker movement are country style too, with simple

above Country style does not have to be based on past traditions. Modern country is epitomized by pale, neutral colours, and a clever juxtaposition of objects, such as this nautical photograph placed next to a model ship.

right This modern country bedroom in Padstow, Cornwall, is in a hotel owned by chef and restaurateur Rick Stein. Textiles have been kept to a minimum, and those that are used provide a strong textural contrast to the otherwise dominant areas of wood.

patterns and a preponderance of wood. This is an ascetic country style of plain walls and floors, with one or two pieces of polished wooden furniture designed for practicality and exemplifying the virtues of sober good taste. There will be natural fibres coloured with vegetable dyes, and on the bed a blanket rather than a duvet.

global styles

Are we more taken with the idea of global decoration than our forefathers? Certainly the art and artifacts brought back by the great explorers and traders of the eighteenth and nineteenth centuries soon filtered into the fashionable decorative consciousness – think of the eighteenth-century fashion for all things Chinese and Indian, from wall coverings to ceramics, or of the late nineteenth-century fashion for everything Japanese.

But we are all world travellers now; indeed our world is so easily accessible that it might be supposed that we have lost our appetite for the decorative style of other lands. But, oddly enough, mass tourism and open-ended worldwide communication seem to have had exactly the opposite effect: so many more of us now travel overseas, seeing and sampling for ourselves the exotic and the romantic, and we want to bring those things back with us. This yearning for the romance of different ways of life is hardly surprising, and where better to re-create it, once home, than in the room of fantasy – the place of sleep and dreams?

Successful transference of global style lies not in attempting to use every element, but rather in extrapolating the key elements of a particular style. In our omnipresent global economy, decorative items from other cultures can be found on every high street – some kitsch, some wonderful, and some exciting when displayed in isolation, but too much when mixed in confusion with everything else. So rigorous editing, as always in interior decoration, is essential. But equally, half-hearted measures do not work: it should be clear to the most casual of observers which particular look you are trying to achieve.

The other mistake to be avoided at all costs when trying out different global styles is to transpose a look that is associated with one climate to a quite

left This wood-lined room is complemented by two beds simply constructed from weathered planks. This rough-hewn quality is another feature associated with country style.

above In this beamed room, a simple nineteenth-century iron bed has been painted a soft colour to match the wall, then dressed with a simple lace cover. A small rug is all that is then required on the polished board floor.

different one. The simple charm of your holiday bedroom on a Greek island during that long summer: the rough, white-painted plaster, bare, polished red-tiled floor, and diaphanous white curtains tumbling in the sea breeze just may not translate quite so well into your north-facing room in a built-up urban environment. Try to match like with like as much as you can or, failing that, just use the elements that travel – a terracotta floor but with a pretty rug, plaster painted a warm-toned white rather than a blinding ice-white, and sheer curtains over a light-reducing blind.

Generally speaking, a particular global style can be created through the associations we make when we see a decorative scheme that awakens memories of other places and times. Possibly the most suggestive element is colour: either consciously or subconsciously we associate different colour palettes with different countries and ways of life, so that a room decorated in a global style could, in theory, be achieved simply by using classical furniture and colour palettes that are instantly evocative of the style.

These could include the cool, pale, clear colours of a Scandinavian-inspired scheme – white, cream, blue, yellow, and a watery *eau-de-nil* – all the colours that make the most of the brief daylight of the north and reflect its pale sun. Or, very different in tone and associations would be the exuberant and rich reds, golds, and blacks of a typical imperial Russian palette, or perhaps the bright, sharp, boiled-sweet colours of the Caribbean, colours that come to life against a backdrop of turquoise sea, hot blue sky, and jungle-green vegetation.

The colours indelibly associated with Africa tend to be those of the heat, the land, and the sky: hot yellows, dense blacks, and earth reds and browns. These colours can be created with the rich, ceremonial tones of *kente* cloth, the woven strips patterned in an infinite variety of geometric designs. In complete contrast, a scheme might be devised around the tones associated with northern French style – a distinctive grey mixed with a touch of fawn; a dull pink, blue or green; and a creamy off-white highlighted with a little gold. In complete contrast to both the preceding palettes are the hot, strong pinks, mustard and saffron yellows, and electric blues and greens of the Indian

above Scandinavian style seems to enjoy perennial popularity. This rural-style Swedish room contains an antique box bed in painted pine which incorporates a storage chest at its foot.

right More sophisticated in tone, but still unmistakably Scandinavian in design, this starkly simple bedroom has pale tones on the walls, which act as a background for the two dramatic, painted beds, each decorated with ribbons.

subcontinent. Any of these distinctive combinations used decoratively in a room would immediately inspire a strong visual connection with the chosen countries and cultures.

Textiles are the other major element associated with specific national decorative styles, and they will add considerable depth to your basic global theme. In a room hung with the scenic charms of a two-toned *toile de Jouy* pattern, one of the traditional designs that have been produced continuously since the eighteenth century, the whole interior scheme would be unmistakably French. Or consider the traditional small regular prints of Provence, in deep red, bright yellow, and blue or black: for many these carry an instant association with the wild rosemary and thyme, pine trees, and lavender of southern France. Equally, window-pane checks in linen, coloured in soft blues and corals, are reliably reminiscent of a Scandinavian interior, while lengths of gold-embroidered sari silks hung around a bed or at a window, or bright woven *madras* checks on cushions and chairs evoke the sights and sounds of India. The individual designs used for the pieced quilts made by early American settlers became so popular and widely recognized that many

far left Since Marco Polo first returned to Venice from the Orient in the late thirteenth century, the influence of eastern taste within international styles has been ever-present. Here, a red-posted, canopied bed has been hung with tassels in the Chinese fashion.

left Asian style is infinitely adaptable. This low bed draped with an eastern textile is surrounded by decorative accessories, all eastern in nature, down to the lampshade in the shape of a Chinese peasant's hat and the scrolls used as wall hangings.

above The rich colours and patterns of India are evoked in this bedroom – influences emphasized by the bold, bright textile wall hanging behind the low bed and the painted table at the bed's foot.

of them were given names, such as Bear's Paw, Flying Geese, and Log Cabin, redolent of their makers' untamed natural surroundings and their physically demanding lives. A room featuring one of these quilt designs can hardly fail to conjure up the environment of rural nineteenth-century America.

The way we think of these different national and cultural styles is idealized and romantic, and our visual memory is usually rooted in whichever period is considered retrospectively to have been most decoratively successful. There are few Scandinavians today living in houses with bleached wooden floors, and distressed wooden chairs painted in grey and gold and decorated with a slip-cover of checked fabric. Or think of the small, steep-roofed rural houses with french windows opening directly on to a terrace, or nineteenth-century apartments with high ceilings and panelled walls painted in a soft grey and outlined with gold leaf fillets – these are our romantic ideals, redolent only of a particular time, and not of a defining national style. Yet there is no reason why such idealized versions of particular places should not inform our personal decorative style. Visual ideas may be drawn from any source: the challenge is to combine them successfully.

above   The cowboy style celebrates the energy of the Wild West. This unusual wooden bed, with its depictions of cowboy life at head and foot, is surrounded with Western artifacts and lit by a rawhide lamp on a burl wood base.

right   An ethnic global style can be achieved through the judicious use of textiles, the design and weave of which conjure up craft traditions and designs from all parts of the world. This room combines textiles and rugs to achieve a warm, eastern look.

far right   The way to San José is clearly shown in this bedroom inspired by Spanish Colonial style. A well-designed room will always have a visual focal point to which the eye is drawn: in this case the group of dolls and pictures above the wooden chest.

overleaf   This bedroom is strongly influenced by the design and motifs of ancient Egypt and by the late nineteenth-century vogue for eastern elements. The painted posts echo the striking decorative panels on the walls.

If you feel inclined to mix different cultures or countries together, this can work well, as long as you abide by the rules of balance and contrast in relation to colour, objects, and pattern. After all, many of the world's greatest collectors have made a point of grouping together their objects, textiles, and curiosities in a pleasing and visually striking way, so that each piece complements its neighbour. These juxtapositions work best when the contrasts are easy to identify at first glance – perhaps a brightly coloured piece of embroidered Chinese silk over a modern, Italian chair or stool; or a carved wooden African figure standing on a low, neo-classically inspired column. Alongside considerations such as these, don't lose sight of the fact that your bedroom should give you lasting pleasure. You must decide what to have where, and ultimately you shouldn't be inhibited by ingrained traditions, design rules, and familiar formulas, because any decorating and furnishing decisions are naturally a question of personal interpretation and taste.

contemporary styles

We have now stepped into the twenty-first century. How the new century will develop stylistically we cannot yet be sure, but it has started on an upbeat note of confidence: the late twentieth century's rather hard-edged minimalism has already given way to a softer, much less severe look, which nevertheless still remains intrinsically simple.

To those who feel nervous about the very thought of contemporary design, fearing that it may be too difficult to live with or too uncompromising, then please think again. Contemporary design is largely about using materials in an interesting way, using space cleverly, and finding new solutions for old problems. There is no single defining look, but instead a hundred variations on current themes – from the sophisticated to the eccentric, and from the elegant to the industrial – all of which can be deployed to striking effect in the contemporary bedroom.

far left The clear light and colours of the Mediterranean are irresistibly appealing, particularly for those who live in cooler climes. A bedroom designed in a Mediterranean style will usually have soft tones and natural textures.

left An absence of colour creates an impression of coolness, whatever the weather. Although here it is a practical necessity, a mosquito net can look equally striking as a purely decorative bed canopy. This effect works best in rural or more unsophisticated surroundings.

right Here strong light is filtered and diffused through the narrow-slatted venetian blind. The bed, meanwhile, is dressed with a tight-fitting cover, and to add the right Mediterranean flavour it is finished with a tailored bolster with tassels.

above left Strong contemporary interiors can encompass any number of classical and traditional references. In this London bed and bathroom designed by architects Juan Corbella and Harper Mackay, a central partition unit separates the bathing area from the bed. Facing the bed, wooden pilasters emphasize the upward movement of the entire scheme.

above right This striking four-poster bed in carved wood also shown above left, has been given air and space, with nothing but a white screen behind to contain it.

right A simple contemporary design incorporating references to both the traditional (the built-in bed head) and eastern style (the raised wooden base). The low table complements the scheme perfectly.

far right The quality of light is critical to the contemporary interior. In the bedroom of Janie Jackson of design company Parma Lilac, the windows are fitted with clever Perspex shutters that offer privacy as well as gently diffused daylight.

The best modern schemes give a sense of space, even when that space is small. Clever use of colour is one effective tool, and telling use of texture is another. For many minimal purists, uncluttered spaces are the only habitable ones – such homes have all their practical necessities hidden behind doors, with only the essential and the beautiful on display within seemingly endless stretches of plain surface. For these purists, every element must justify its presence, and no superfluous clutter will be tolerated.

Surfaces count for a great deal in the contemporary bedroom, sometimes hard-edged, but (ideally) always tempered with textural candy – suede or velvet perhaps, or thick woollen blankets. Although these surfaces can be inexpensive, they certainly shouldn't look it. The hard/soft equation often centres around the appearance of the bed itself, where the geometric proportions are often emphasized and then softened with a headboard covered in a luxurious material, or a quantity of rich and contrasting pillows. This is a bedroom where new technology plays a critical role, but is not always visible. In the same way as some fashion pundits maintain that a well-dressed woman's clothes should never be ostentatious or obstrusive, so too the technological wonders of the contemporary bedroom should perform their magic unseen.

A contemporary purist bedroom does not necessarily require age and tradition to be banished from within its walls. A quiet new elegance can be achieved through the reinterpretation of a traditional look. Indeed, many of the most successful contemporary schemes incorporate antique or ethnic pieces, although used in a precise and thoughtful manner, with each piece viewed as an object in its own right, rather than being just another piece of furniture. An interesting bed could play this role: an ornate, antique four-poster might be reinterpreted, for instance, by being pruned back to its basic framework with no hangings at all, or merely with simple gauze slips at every corner. Alternatively, if the room is large enough, an old day bed or chaise longue covered in bright, deckchair stripes could be the perfect accessory.

Although there are many who equate pure contemporary style with pale, neutral colours or no colour at all, this does not mean that brighter, stronger colours have to be excluded from the modern bedroom. Bold colours can

left This design by architect Simon Condor demonstrates an ingenious use of space. The bedroom is a self-contained private retreat yet a real sense of freedom is created by the glass walls, which give the impression of being open to the skies.

above This tall room divider stops just short of being an internal wall, and serves to partition the living area from the sleeping area. The bed itself is a self-contained haven of comfort, from its faux-fur-covered headboard to the comprehensive lighting system controlled from the bedside panel.

overleaf The bedroom of interior designer Kate Earle, of company Todhunter Earle, is a warm, affectionate take on a classic style reinterpreted in a simple, modern manner. The emphasis is on texture, comfort, and warm, soft tones.

support kitsch and eccentric interior styles – contemporary interpretations that are diametrically opposed to muted minimalism. Grey and black tones can also work well in bedrooms, although they are most successful as touches of drama rather than as the dominant shades. Slashes of deep brown can also be effective, particularly in a neutral scheme, where the brown adds richness and depth to the paler shades.

If you choose to use pale colours or an all-neutral palette, then add textural interest through a careful choice of surfaces that will lend contrast and energy to what could otherwise tend towards the bland. The technique of using a number of whites and off-whites together on woodwork and walls is as fresh today as it was in the period following the Second World War when the decorator John Fowler designed schemes using up to ten different shades of white. Although it can be difficult to achieve just the right degree of subtlety, an immense variety of white and off-white shades is now available from specialist paint manufacturers.

Many of the elements treasured by lovers of contemporary style follow a direct line of descent from the decorative bedroom schemes of the mid

above This muted bedroom with very deliberately placed furnishings exudes an aura of harmony and calmness. Distracting elements that would disturb the low key mood are avoided.

right With every surface gleaming with silvery sophistication, this bedroom is a polished tribute to 1930s glamour. Such a scheme should remain focused, so that nothing is allowed to distract from it.

left Designer Andrew Logan's bedroom is a seemingly haphazard combination of objects and styles. Such an eclectic mix requires considerable skill and discipline, however, particularly in the choice of colours and textures.

left This striking bedroom belonging to artist Dougie Fields, is as much a showcase for art as a resting place. The ornate fireplace acts as a striking head and surround for the low bed.

right Eccentric and unique, this bedroom wittily mixes classical and traditional taste with twenty-first-century style. Against a strong, Jacobean-style wallpaper, a towering gilded headboard of chivalric proportions complements a bed covered with a patriotic pieced satin quilt.

far right A different view of the room shown to the right. Throughout the room pictures, quirky decorative objects, and pieces of furniture are displayed in amusing juxtaposition.

twentieth century. This elegant look based on tactile textures and textiles (such as suede, silk, and velvet), sensual luxury, comfort, and escape is the epitome of modernity. Colours to fit with this style are pale: watery pinks and lilacs, greys, and greens that exemplify the sophisticated pastel glamour of the Mayfair and Manhattan hotels of the 1920s. This sensual style is reflective: surfaces sparkle and gilded mirrors abound. Gentle lighting glimmers throughout with a number of small lamps bathing the whole space in light. The floor would be soft underfoot – flat-weave carpets or rugs in pale tones positioned on light, rather than dark, wooden boards. This style denies the elegance of frills and ribbons, although lines do not have to be too severe, and rounded edges or pleats can be used.

In startling contrast, but certainly part of the same canon, is what might be called "contemporary bold." This is the style of the outrageous, mixing both old and new unashamedly, in a way that is both contemporary and timeless. This modern look is about the unexpected: the surprise of textural contrasts, the magic of combined colours, and the sheer delight of the unconventional. New and old work together and the decoration is exuberant, taking risks where other schemes would be more pedestrian. Each of the bedrooms illustrated within this genre, however, although joyous in spirit and free in appearance, has been put together with deliberation, care, and discipline. Even more relevant than with other manifestations of contemporary decorative style, the ultimate success of the eccentric modern style depends on achieving a sensitive balance.

bedroom treatments

Research shows that people simply do not get enough sleep – fifty per cent of us have sleep patterns that adversely affect our health. How you arrange your bedroom can not only speed the rate at which you fall asleep, but also increase the quality of your sleeping hours. The perfect bedroom should be comfortable, of course, and well organized, with everything in its place. It should also be so enticing and welcoming that it radiates sleep-inducing serenity.

previous pages The four-poster bed is a style that is recognized and coveted worldwide. The unadorned simplicity of these two single four-poster beds has a distinctly eastern flavour.

left Interior designer Mimi O'Connell incorporated a metal-framed bed with an airy corona in this Tuscan room. In order not to detract from the bed's lines, she refrained from using any hangings and combined it with a strong table and mirror.

right This ornate iron bed has been placed like a throne between a pair of ornate upright chairs. The symmetrical composition is framed by a pair of imposing columns, also in perfect symmetry.

The word "comfortable" derives from the Latin *confortare*, which means to strengthen. By the eighteenth century the meaning of the word had developed to include the sense of physical well-being that we use it to describe. The bed should unarguably be the quintessence of comfort, no matter what space it occupies and how regularly it is used. Do not let your spare bedroom house a bed in which your guests will pass one of those endless, restless nights where their every toss and turn unearths a new bump, dip, or uncomfortable furrow.

bed types

You need to choose a bed that suits you and the style of your bedroom. The multiplicity of styles and designs available can seem overwhelming, but in fact they all belong to the four main types of bed that have developed over the centuries. These consist of the tester or four-poster bed; the couch or day bed with enclosed sides; the divan, at its simplest a mattress on top of a base; and the ubiquitous standard single bed with either metal or wooden ends. Almost every bed style today whether antique or modern, plain or decorative, and however much embellished, expanded, and redesigned is derived from one of these four early models.

The first posted or tester beds are recorded in the early sixteenth century. These models were crude, with simple posts at each corner of the bed frame supporting the full- or half-length canopy or tester that gave the bed its name. This basic shape developed considerably over the next two hundred years, with emphasis given alternately to the posts and the hangings. A variation on this basic shape was the half-tester, in which the canopy extended over only half the length of the bed.

Modern tastes still incline towards beds framed with posts, despite the fact that we no longer need to enclose ourselves within curtains to protect us from draughts, block out the light, and ensure privacy in an overcrowded room. In addition to the traditional ornate treatments, there are now many modern interpretations of four-poster bed styles tending towards simpler and more restrained designs. Such beds often have no hangings at all, allowing a better appreciation of the architectural form of the four-poster. If your four-poster is antique, and elaborately carved or otherwise decorated, then losing the dressing could give the bed a new lease of life.

The second influential form of bed was encased or enfolded in polished or painted wood. This bed developed from a couch or day bed and by the eighteenth century had evolved into such imaginative variations as the French *bateau lit*, the Russian sleigh bed, and the neo-classical canopied couch.

These beds were often crowned with a dome or draped hanging, of which many variations were produced in Empire France and Regency England.

This type of bed has now regained much of its original popularity. Modern reproductions may be chosen as much for their visual charm as for the fact that they provide a comfortable place to sleep. A bed of this type is particularly effective in a bedroom that is used in the day; set against a wall, it can be dressed with a bolster running the length of the bed, with additional small bolsters or cushions at head and foot.

The third shape, and perhaps the most universally popular, is the divan. This consists of a simple mattress, thick or thin, set on or within a base, often without a head- or footboard. Variations on this bed form appear in all cultures and countries. Should you prefer this more straightforward alternative, there is no end to the possible variations on the theme. The mattress may be shallow

far left Many four-poster beds have decorated or carved posts. Where these are made of hard, cold materials, such as the metal posts seen here, then elements of softness should be introduced: in this case in the form of a full, luxuriant bedcover that tempers their starkness.

left A bamboo four-poster is an elegant and lighthearted take on traditional models. The rest of the room has been kept simple and uncluttered – often the best response to such a strong bed shape.

right This bedroom, designed by Maja Walters and Michael Reeves, features a regal bed with fine posts. All that is needed to dress it are a luxurious white cover and an airy, light-diffusing curtain.

or deep with a wide or narrow base, while the headboards may be insignificant or substantial and fixed to either a base or a wall. If you have a conventional mattress on a matching base, think carefully about its position and how it is styled. Is it standing in the most interesting position within the room? Could it run along the wall instead of against it? Would it look better boxed in, surrounded by shelves or other storage space? Might it look better curtained? And for a more modern look, what about the mattress on its own, set on top of a box-shaped base that, with the addition of drawers, could also provide alternative storage? And look at using unconventional bedspreads and covers – perhaps a mixture of old and ethnic textiles.

Although metal beds made of brass or iron are widely regarded as a Victorian invention, John Evelyn, the indefatigable English seventeenth-century diarist, remarked on them in Italy some two hundred years earlier. It was not until the nineteenth century, however, following the 1851 Great Exhibition, that tubular metal beds were manufactured in large quantities. Their popularity in this period is attributed to the belief at this time that metal bedsteads were more hygienic than wooden ones, because they gave less sanctuary for the bed bugs that plagued the Victorians.

There is a wide choice of metal-ended beds now available. Although the originals and historical reproductions still look good, the decorative mood has moved away from the use of rounded, shiny brass to the slightly subtler look of matt ironwork. Many metal beds can also be painted, and matt colours tend to look better than high-shine ones. Avoid primary and violently bright shades, using instead soft greens, silver greys, air-force blues, even dusky lilacs: colours that will subtly emphasize the curved charms of the bed. You may wish to underscore the nineteenth-century style with a simple, closely patterned wallpaper and a polished wooden floor. Alternatively, the clean lines of a metal bed would look good against a background of clean colour and simple blinds.

left This London penthouse loft by Block Architecture is a highly modern statement, with a bed that combines elements of both the traditional four-poster and the built-in bed. The slatted surround manages to give both privacy and a sense of air and space.

overleaf Designed by John Lautner in 1982, this Los Angeles bedroom has a simple, timeless quality. Tatami mats sit on a base of Douglas fir timber, which also holds deep storage drawers. A floor of rough-cut stone makes a cool contrast with the wood surfaces.

above The extravagant carved wooden intricacies of this Victorian Gothic tester bed, in a bedroom designed by Tessa Kennedy, are wisely unobscured by the folds of bed curtains. Only the canopy has been lined in a simple cream fabric.

bed heads and headboards

The headboard developed from the piece of cloth that in early medieval times hung from the canopy to drape the wall behind the sleeper's head. Early headboards were fine wooden objects, with earlier models carved, painted, and decorated and later ones inventively and decoratively upholstered. During the twentieth century, the headboard degenerated into an overblown, padded, buttoned, frilled, and flowered appendage, often quite out of proportion to the bed it adorned. This was unfortunate, as such designs lost the impact of the headboard as a valuable part of a comfortable bed.

The principal practical use of a headboard is as a backrest, providing support for the occupant's back when sitting up in bed and a non-sliding surface on which pillows can rest. Headboards also fulfill an aesthetic function, defining the bed space, and imparting a feeling of containment and enclosure. So why not add a headboard to a simple bed? It doesn't have to be bought ready made, as plywood panels can be covered with material, and this an ideal way to display a small piece of antique fabric, an old paisley shawl, a length of embroidered Chinese silk, or a piece of ornate beading and embroidery. Other ideas for headboards include an old shutter turned on its side with the moulding coloured to match the decorative scheme, a panel of painted canvas, or even a piece of wallpaper pasted on a panel of wood. Custom-made headboards can be visual features in their own right, and may be designed to incorporate improbable feats of technology, allowing you to command lighting, sound, and vision systems from a remote-control panel.

A headboard does not even have to be attached to the bed, but rather can work as a form of artistic punctuation. Something hung behind the bed to draw the eye can have as much decorative value as a more conventional solution.

far left The wall behind the bed provides many decorative opportunities. This room makes imaginative use of a graphic nineteenth-century poster, which acts as the main focal point of the room. Every element, from the textiles to the pictures, uses the same colour palette.

middle left Interior designer Vivien Roberts has created a rich, luxurious atmosphere in this bedroom by using a lavender wallpaper with a design of delicately swaying trees on the wall at the head of the bed.

left Architects Tsao and McKown have used the wall space behind and above this bed as a surface on which to display decorative objects and an abstract photograph, creating a group that echoes the vibrant yellow quilt below.

far left A pared-down example of the combination of form and function. The high headboard has two elegant, swan-necked reading lights set above it, which lend a slight organic flourish to offset the strong vertical and horizontal lines.

left Curved and commanding, this arching wooden bedhead would dominate a room of any size. The warm wood encloses the bed beneath and reflects the glow of the reading lights placed on the matching wooden side tables.

above left An ingenious storage solution incorporates a padded headboard, in soft contrast to the sharp lines of the built-in shelves, cupboards, and drawers surrounding the bed.

above right This antique bed has a carved wooden structure with head- and footboards. The flowing, curved lines of the end pieces are faithfully followed by a simple cream fabric covering.

left Somewhere between a half-tester and a *lit à la turque*, this formal curtain arrangement gathers bed drapes that flow past the bedhead to fall generously on the floor. Lined and interlined, they offer a warm contrast to the figured floral cotton on the rest of the bed.

A picture hung low, a relatively one-dimensional sculpture, or indeed a hanging such as a tapestry, a quilt, or a small rug would all provide contemporary takes on the original medieval bedhead.

bed hangings

When the design of the bedstead was in its infancy, the hangings surrounding it were imaginatively luxurious. This is clearly demonstrated with surviving fragments of historic textiles and inventories listing such hangings in minute detail, and recording the sumptuous use of velvet, silk, tapestry, fur, and gold and silver thread. By the eighteenth century, lighter woods were being used to make beds and bed hangings became correspondingly lighter in weight. Diarists and commentators of the seventeenth and eighteenth centuries often noted the hangings and furnishings of the bedrooms they stayed in, detailing many an opulent collection of textures. Designs of this period frequently featured domes or small canopies. A dome suspended centrally from the ceiling was known as a *lit à la polonaise*, while fixed to the wall it became a *lit à l'anglaise* or a *lit à la turque*. A full-length tester projecting from the head of the bed was a *lit à la duchesse*, and a half-size tester a *lit à l'ange*.

From these domes and canopies, many of them gilded, lightweight fabrics such as silk, satin, taffeta, and cotton cascaded in drapes, furls, and festoons. Pleated, tied, bunched, and caught with ribbons and ropes, these lighter fabrics marked a distinct departure from the use of dense, heavy velvet and brocade. Now the vogue was for everything light, ethereal, and above all feminine. The use of these canopies and domes above the bed has now regained its popularity. Beds dressed in this way can be pretty, frivolous, and fun – all worthy qualities in a bedroom. A word of caution, however: while a "pretty" bedroom can be quite charming, a pretty style does not depend on a palette of saccharine colours, a froth of elaborate frills and spills in contrasting patterns, or a liberal scattering of heart-shaped, lace-trimmed cushions. If you are using soft, washed-out colours, then balance them with strong shapes. Aim for tailored curtains, plain furniture, and a restricted range of patterns.

above A traditional half-tester or *lit à l'ange*. The strong lines of the heavy canopy embellished with gold are offset by the free-standing bed, which is viewed in profile against the darkness of the canopy.

There should always be an air of luxury about a canopy and bed curtains. As far as the full or half-tester is concerned, the look can easily be achieved without posts. A rectangular frame can be attached to the head of the bed or the wall behind, and the curtains can be hung from this. Should you wish to emulate the *lit à la polonaise*, use a modern corona or crown made from either metal or wood. The metal ones can be garishly bright, so consider ways of distressing them, as a patina of age is always preferable visually. Designed either as a full crown projecting towards the centre of the bed or as a semicircle attached to the wall above the head of the bed, a corona can be draped with silks, cottons, or Indian muslin. You could also use one of the new sheers, the development of which has been one of the great advances in textile manufacture. They are light, airy, and chic, but at the same time extremely hardwearing, and can be washed vigorously and often.

Corona drapes and tester curtains can also be lined on the inside with a contrasting fabric. Make sure that the contrast between the main fabric and lining is not too dramatic and that you like the juxtaposition of fabrics, because this is what you will see when lying in bed.

Another bed fashion once widespread across Europe, particularly in the north, was the enclosed bed, or *lit clos*. Literally a bed in a box, this is a very useful and smart way of combining sleeping and storage. The bed is positioned along the length of a wall, with cupboards and shelves built on either side, above, and even below, so creating a sleeping alcove. A light source should be installed within the alcove, either from above or attached to the head of the bed. Hangings could be added, either as dress curtains or to enclose and hide the bed during the day.

curtains and blinds

If you are considering a fabric-hung bed treatment, always take the window treatment into account. Although neither window curtains nor blinds need to match the bed curtains exactly, they should none the less complement or relate to the bed in some way – through style, colour or design. Even if you have decided against any formal bed treatment, your curtains should reflect

above A traditional style of four-poster can also accommodate a simple fabric dressing. The lattice-work inside the canopy and behind the head of the bed and the unfussy curtain treatment demonstrate the contemporary origins of the design.

right Bed curtains and drapes do not have to be elaborate or expensive. Here, material has been draped over the frame of the tester and made into curtains at each post.

above left In this bedroom under the eaves, an antique Empire bed, complete with ormolu decoration, is enhanced by a small central canopy over which curtains are draped from head to foot. The effect is enhanced by the pleated fabric used to drape the walls.

left Transported from their humble origins, these twin metal beds are crowned with simple, wall-hung drapes that endow them with a sense of occasion.

far left A wall-hung half-corona can be so dramatic in its impact that it hardly needs any further dressing. This example uses a sheer, unlined fabric that leaves the bed relatively unadorned.

above Choosing a bed to match its architectural surroundings can be a challenge. This bed within an arched alcove does this by using a half corona that extends behind the bed towards the highest point of the space.

above If the bed hangings use sheer fabrics, a successful scheme will complement the diaphanous, light-filled effect that they create with window dressings in a similar vein. A material such as a heavy, dark velvet, by contrast, would overwhelm the lighter fabric.

right This antique day bed has been simply dressed so that its elegant lines are fully visible. At its head, narrow white curtains hang from a demure corona. The whole is a lesson in restraint.

the cover you have chosen, whether this is a duvet or a bedspread. While bedrooms are not now upholstered and curtained in the same material throughout as they were in the seventeenth century, remember that both bed and windows are part of the same overall decorative scheme, and should be considered in combination.

As far as style is concerned, bedroom curtains are the most appropriate opportunity to indulge in extravagant creations of flamboyant or feminine fabrics. That said, don't forget that femininity should not be confused with fussiness. Stay away from very busy patterns, if you want flowers then keep them simple, and avoid frills, bows, or other ornamental additions. This is not to prohibit the use of chintz in the bedroom. With its repeating patterns of large flowers and richly plumed, exotic birds, this elegant fabric has long been the traditional choice for bedrooms. Many fabric reproductions of document prints from the eighteenth and nineteenth centuries are now available, as well as clean, contemporary versions of older designs.

While bedroom curtains should look attractive, they should also fulfil the practical functions of insulation and blocking out the light. There is nothing more annoying than a curtain that is not quite long or full enough, through which the morning light regularly infiltrates. Bedroom curtains should be lined, and sometimes interlined too. If you want to have a lightweight fabric in a pale colour or design, then it can be a good idea to fit blinds as well – either conventional ones or specially treated black-out blinds (also available in colours other than black).

The bedroom window is the perfect place to use lightweight, sheer curtains, in fabrics such as muslin, voile, lawn, and lightweight silk. These fabrics can be highly decorative (embroidered, figured, printed), or alternatively can simply be used in pretty, plain lengths. Voluminous, full-length curtains made from an abundance of sheer fabric have a luxurious air of fragile femininity. Hang them from a metal or wooden pole, or behind a deep pelmet covered in a contrasting fabric. Sheers can also be used in conjunction with a light-excluding roller blind, generally smarter in white than in black or blue. These also look good combined with dress curtains: another case where

left In a tiny room with a small window, effective use of natural light is all important. In this attic bedroom, hinged curtain rods have been used to allow the rod and curtain to swing back into the reveal and not obscure the window.

right In a Manhattan apartment designed by Pierce Allen, the bedroom has two walls of windows. In order to avoid the otherwise inevitable glare, each window has been generously hung with full, sheer curtains. The resulting diffused light gives the whole room a soft, warm glow.

far right Day beds (this is a typical late eighteenth-century example) were designed to be used as lounging beds during the day, and should be dressed with comfortable cushions and bolsters. In a dual-purpose living space, this is a period version of a contemporary sofa bed.

a black-out blind is needed. Never be too economical when calculating the quantity of material required for sheer curtains – too little fabric with such a lightweight structure will look ungenerous and inadequate.

Blinds are an increasingly popular option for bedroom windows. Whether they are roller, roman, venetian, roll-up split cane, or bamboo, their clean lines work well with contemporary decorative schemes, and they can often be much more effective than curtains in a small bedroom. If you decide to use roller blinds, give careful consideration to both the design and weight of the fabric you choose. Some fabrics need to be stiffened professionally in order to give them the extra body necessary to hang well, and this could result in a change in texture and appearance. Some fabric designs work better than others for blinds – large floral prints would not be as successful as plain colours or geometric designs, for example.

Roman blinds have a sharper structure than roller blinds. Originally popular in the eighteenth century, they have a useful role in contemporary settings, particularly on larger windows where a roller blind can look unbalanced. When let down, a roman blind lies almost against the window, and when not in use it draws up into wide, flat, horizontal pleats. These look particularly effective as they are set inside the window frame and expose the surrounding wooden architrave, which can be painted to contrast with the blind.

Other types of blinds include venetian blinds, known in France as *jalousies à la persienne*. Originally made from wood, these can be found today in a variety of materials – including plastic or metal as well as wood – with slats of different widths. If you want to create an oriental or tropical look, consider using blinds made from finely split cane or bamboo, which are moderately priced and produced in a wide variety of colours.

pillows and sheets

The perfect bedroom will naturally have perfect bedlinen – pillows, sheets, and blankets, or duvets. Sheets have a long history: fragments discovered originating from Ancient Egypt and Rome show that linen could be woven as finely 2,000 years ago as it is today. If you are looking for luxurious cotton sheets, then it is the thread count that makes the difference. The higher the thread count (the number of threads there are to the inch), the finer and softer the sheet and the higher the price.

There are many different types of sheet; if you prefer sheets that need a minimum of ironing, then choose those made from a mixture of synthetic and natural fibres, or alternatively you might prefer to have brushed cotton sheets with a slightly furry texture. Some prefer the cool frostiness of linen: more expensive than cotton, linen sheets come in different qualities, of which the price is the general indication. Linen becomes softer with age, and linen sheets can last a lifetime. This explains why beautifully monogrammed antique linen sheets can still be found in antique shops and markets, and at auction sales. Always measure the dimensions of antique linen sheets before buying them to make sure they will fit your beds, as nineteenth-century beds were both shorter and narrower than modern ones. Even if an attractive old linen sheet is too short to use as a top or bottom sheet, however, it could still be used as a crisp, stylish bed cover.

The main decision when choosing bedlinen is between an all-white colour scheme and a mixed palette of colours. If you favour white bed linen, then ensure that it is always brilliantly fresh. If white is not your taste, then consider cool, pale colours – neutrals such as grey and taupe, or geometric patterns. These tend to be easier to live with than linen with masses of multi-coloured blooms.

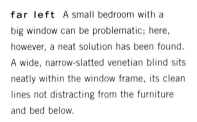

far left A small bedroom with a big window can be problematic; here, however, a neat solution has been found. A wide, narrow-slatted venetian blind sits neatly within the window frame, its clean lines not distracting from the furniture and bed below.

left In this Spanish house, a blind has been used to make a clever division between a bedroom and its bathroom. The narrow doorway has been hung with a rattan blind, so that it marks the entrance without blocking the light.

right Sophisticated and masculine, this bedroom in the St Martins Lane Hotel in London, designed by French designer Philippe Starck, is decorated in off-white. The wooden-slatted blinds at the window are teamed with heavy curtains in a dusky grey. The overall impression is one of comfortable relaxation.

above In a contemporary interior, a clean, incisive look can be achieved with the right bedlinen. Here, on a burnt orange bed base, the sheets, pillows, and blankets form the main visual features of the bedroom scheme.

above right This bedlinen in a muted floral design introduces a soft, romantic dimension to the room. To look coherent, the theme should be carried through in other elements of the design.

right A bed inspired by the undoubtedly less glamorous hospital trolley is dressed immaculately with crisp bedlinen, the quilt tucked in smartly to create an air of efficiency and order.

far right This bedroom in Majorca provides a cool haven from the heat of the day. The upholstered scroll-end beds and the bedlinen are a cool combination of pale greys and white.

above A bedroom showing how clichés can be reinvented. In the style of a 1930s Hollywood boudoir, this room focuses on silky textures, thick rugs, and the four gold-headed figures surrounding the bed.

You may choose to to keep soft piles of pillows and bolsters on your bed – a device that rarely fails to make the bed seem more luxurious and welcoming. However many you decide to have, always buy the best that you can afford, and plump them up regularly to make the bed more inviting. There are pillows to suit every taste, stuffed with materials from Hungarian goose down, to firm, hypo-allergenic synthetics. The thickness of a pillow should equal the length of the sleeper's shoulder; so supporting the neck, and giving the spinal chord the most comfortable curvature for sleeping. Pillows should be replaced, or at least washed, every three years. Some health professionals advise doing this every six months, particularly for those who are allergic to dust, in order to avoid an accumulation of house dust mites. Synthetic pillows should also be washed occasionally, to disperse the dust and the oil that collects on them.

Modern bedrooms can accommodate either sheets and blankets or duvets. Choose the option that best suits your bedroom. A pared-down, trim bed will suit sheets and blankets tucked in tightly rather than a big padded duvet, and many of the range of new blanket designs are stylish enough not to need hiding beneath a cover. Equally, if you favour a cosy, relaxed, informal style, the bed might look better submerged beneath the inviting folds of a plump, billowing duvet.

The bedroom is the one place in your home where you should have complete freedom to indulge your fantasies, so take your pick from the various ideas profiled here, as well as from the practical suggestions outlined in the Essentials chapter, on pages 142–167. Whether you are ordering a new bed in an unconventional shape, looking for ways to disguise a standard single bed with lengths of dramatic fabric, planning to rethink the style of your curtains and fabric dressings, or searching for a headboard that will complement your simple divan, then make your choices with confidence. This is the essence of any successful bedroom – a sensitive combination of brio and personal style.

right Designer Andrew Logan always avoids taking a conventional, obvious style route. In his regal bedroom, the bed is dressed in a rich red cover and a gold-spangled canopy is draped the length of the bed.

overleaf This spectacular rounded room is in the Palais Bulles (Bubble Palace) in Cap d'Antibes, designed by architect Antti Lovag for Pierre Cardin in the 1980s. There are no straight lines or angles within any of the rooms: each wall is curved and the bed itself is rounded.

lighting & storage

Lighting and storage may seem mundane when compared with other, apparently more glamorous, areas of design, such as the arrangement of space and the fine details of style. The fact reamains, mevertheless, that these are the two most important elements in bedroom design. Get them right and everything else will fall gently, and satisfyingly, into place.

previous pages This bed at the St Martins Lane Hotel in London, designed by Philippe Starck, is set into an alcove that has atmospheric, concealed down-lighters and wall-mounted reading lights at exactly the right height. The light from the down-lighters can be adjusted to blue, green, yellow, or purple, according to the whim of the guest.

left Soft, natural daylight is the standard that artificial lighting aims to emulate. Recent technical and electrical advances have brought artificial lighting nearer to achieving this goal than before.

right Sometimes even natural light can be too much, particularly when the sun is at its most dazzling. Well-designed blinds can diffuse and control the light, allowing it to be adjusted according to requirements.

When planning how to light a room, remember the two basic principles: natural lighting should have equal importance to artificial lights, and the most effective artificial light is as soft and subtle as its natural counterpart. This is particularly true in the bedroom, where it goes without saying that harsh, extreme light conditions are inappropriate.

The first step is to decide how much you would like to spend on artificial lights. Whether you are looking for basic, functional pieces, or expensive designer lights, there is a diverse range of models from which to choose. At one level, competitively priced models can be sourced from a local hardware shop, and at the other a lighting designer could be commissioned to plan and install the latest technological developments. Several different methods of lighting are desirable in a bedroom, varying according to the way the room is used. Task lighting is targeted at specific uses such as reading in bed, applying make up, and studying, while more general background lighting should create a subdued, relaxing atmosphere. The colour of the bedroom walls will also affect how much lighting is needed, so bear in mind that dark tones absorb light, and pale colours reflect it.

Tungsten and halogen are the principal types of light used in the bedroom. Tungsten is a traditional, soft, and gold-tinted light, while halogen light is newer, crisper, and whiter. If you decide to mix them, tungsten light is perfect for warm background lighting, while halogen works well in low- and main-voltage lights. It is especially suitable for task lighting, often working better than traditional tungsten lamps for reading in bed, particularly in fittings mounted on the wall or attached to the bed head.

Many people buy low table lights for bedside reading, yet in fact this is the least comfortable scenario, as you would need to lie flat on your back,

pillowless, for the light to illuminate the page fully. Bedside lights should stand high enough so that when the reader is sitting up in bed the light falls naturally on the book without shining in their face. This is the reason why many people avoid conventional table lights, preferring either adjustable office or desk lights, floor lamps that can be angled, or lights fixed to the wall or bed head. Of course, if two people are sharing a bed or a bedroom, two reading lights are essential, and they should have separate switches.

Background lighting provides the opportunity to introduce more subtle lighting elements in the form of concealed lighting, which can lend a different atmosphere to the room. Some form of up-lighting is a good start, and this can be by means of a device as simple as tubular lights concealed behind pieces of furniture. Other places where light sources can be hidden include the tops of cupboards or storage units and the underside of shelves. The point of concealed lighting is to achieve a diffuse, low, welcoming glow. You can then create a mood ranging from seductive to cosy, depending on your preference and the sophistication of your (essential) dimmer switches. Ensure that you have enough light sources at varying heights, even if you do not use them all

above The bed shown here benefits from both ambient lighting and task lighting: behind the bed is a window with a white blind that creates a soft, diffused light, while at either side are two tall bedside lights. While not strictly high enough for reading in bed, they provide a pleasing symmetry to the scheme.

right A light may be valued purely for its decorative qualities. Napoleon he may not be, but this bust made into a lamp base and topped with a distinctly military shade is amusing and original.

far right The clean lines of this four-poster bed set on a broad wooden base are emphasized by the original background lighting. The deep alcoves on the wall allow in panels of bright natural light which contrast with the shade of the room.

the time; too few sources of light will create the disagreeable effect of deep pools of darkness interspersed with brittle points of contrasting, bright light.

As in every other room, you should be able to switch the lights on from the door. You should also be able to switch them off from the bed. Nothing is more annoying than to realize, just as you are drifting off to sleep, that you will have to get out of bed to turn out the lights.

Task lighting is another essential lighting device for the bedroom, and this means creating enough sources of light for each different bedroom activity. Reading in bed has already been covered, but there are other activities within the bedroom that need effective lighting, such as dressing and undressing. Mirrors and their surrounding areas need a good overall level of light, and dressing tables or mirrors above a chest of drawers should ideally be lit from both sides. Any sort of mirror should be lit as honestly as you dare: soft,

subdued lighting may make you feel better, but it can also hide a dreadful fashion or grooming *faux pas*. Task lighting also includes illuminating cupboards and storage areas. It is exasperating not to be able to see all the contents of a cupboard, and in a fixed wardrobe a light that comes on when the door is open is really useful. So, too, are the small fluorescent strips that run off batteries. These can be fixed anywhere in a room, even at floor level so that you can distinguish easily between your black, brown, and navy blue shoes.

Task lighting serves a useful role in children's bedrooms, as children often use their rooms for very specific activities. They may need adjustable lamps mounted over desks or tables that can swing or be angled to highlight painting, building, or writing projects. A child's room also requires good background lighting that conveys a warm, sunny atmosphere, as well as a strong bedside reading light in order to encourage the reading of books in bed – a habit that,

far left If your room has a centre light, take the time to find a shade that fits the atmosphere of the room. This glowing centre light in the shape of a pear drop suits the simple, restrained style of the bedroom that it lights.

middle left Drop chandeliers are available in many designs – from painted metal to necklaces of coloured glass. They inject an atmosphere of frivolity and femininity into any bedroom.

left Modern lighting can be integrated effectively within traditional settings as well as contemporary ones. Here, antique furniture including a sleigh bed is combined with the sinuous lines of a ceiling-hung, serpentine track system.

overleaf The lighting in this bedroom is as subtle as the colour scheme. Tall reading lights are positioned behind the bed, while other lights are strategically placed around the room to create an atmosphere of subdued sophistication.

once acquired, will stay with them for life. For bedside lamps, conical shades are far better than shallow shades, which can be too glaring.

Accent lighting fulfils a different role from task lighting, being a purely decorative tool to highlight a picture or draw attention to a special object or piece of furniture. This type of lighting is not strictly necessary, but it does give extra texture to the overall lighting scheme, and provides an extra polish that makes the atmosphere of a room memorable. Lights can also be artistic statements. The combination of new materials and light sources developed in recent years has meant that designers are producing lights that are objects of beauty in themselves. Some of these are designed to be centre lights or chandeliers, others to be displayed at table or shelf height, while others again look better at floor level. Wherever they are placed, their purpose is to amuse and enchant, and what more could you wish for in a bedroom?

storage

This is undoubtedly the most important element in the bedroom after the bed. It provides somewhere to put essentials and other objects where they can easily be reached, and in a way that makes the best use of the space. Storage can be provided in many different forms: wardrobes, cupboards or other hanging spaces, shelving, fold-away systems, bedside tables, desks, chests, drawers, boxes and even furniture with built-in storage space.

There is nothing more dispiriting than an untidy bedroom – one where you cannot find anything when you need it, where there is limited hanging space, and where dirty clothes mix with freshly laundered ones. Think about your current bedroom arrangement. Is there anything abandoned in a pile on the floor, are bits and pieces thrown into a catch-all basket or box, or do coats and jackets hang three-deep on a hook at the back of the door? All these

far left The key factor in successful storage is that it should be designed to fit the space that you have available, however awkward that might be. Spaces under sloping roofs, as here, are easily converted into extra storage space.

left In a pretty bedroom decorated in a simple, rural style, a storage system has been constructed using wicker baskets of different dimensions as drawers. Hanging space is incorporated into the system, which has been carefully planned to meet the specific needs of its owner.

right The perfect gentleman's dressing room, fit for the most fastidious beau. Ensuring a place for everything, each element has been designed to exactly the right dimensions – the shelves are shallow enough for precisely one shirt, and ample hanging space means trousers can be graded according to colour and texture.

left A wall of fitted cupboards is not always the most attractive of storage solutions. The answer can be to visually interrupt any large surfaces with decorative details such as mouldings and surface textures.

elements require storage, but the trick is to match the storage to the objects. Storage facilities ideally need to be adapted to each individual, which means that ready-made systems or pieces of furniture are often not the best solution, because they are likely to address a general storage problem rather than your problem in particular.

Different styles of clothing require different storage solutions. You might favour long coats and dresses and therefore require a considerable amount of full-length hanging space, usually calculated at a maximum height of 1.6m (5ft 3in); for someone who prefers a jeans-and-T-shirt style, on the other hand, shallow shelves are a more appropriate solution. There are basic guidelines for general dimensions: shelves for sweaters and shirts should be shallow and many, rather than deep and few, measuring usually 30 x 55cm (1ft x 1ft 10in). Deep shelves tend to result in piles that fall over, while shallow shelves double up as good storage for hats and handbags.

Hanging space is often best divided into two sections, one above and one below. The associated access problems of an upper hanging space have been solved with the introduction of wardrobe lifts: weighted hanging rails that pull

left These fitted cupboards have been designed not as a single flat run along a wall, but rather in staggered units of varying depths. The doors are furnished with large and striking cupboard handles.

above This stretch of cupboards runs across an entire bedroom wall. When open, the different shapes of door reveal spaces with individual combinations of shelves and cupboards. Together these suit the storage of virtually every possible type of clothing and object.

down by means of a central rod. Free-standing wardrobes can be challenging to integrate, as they take up a large amount of space, and are rarely designed to work with your particular clothing problems. The obvious alternative is a fitted wardrobe, or a combination of cupboards and wardrobe, but be careful not to create a wall of unvarying wooden doors. If you would like to follow this format, then break the expanse of doors up with colour, architectural detail, and carefully chosen handles.

If you are having a cupboard built, make it deep enough to hold a full-size coathanger complete with clothes hanging on it – a depth of approximately 60cm (2ft). This sounds obvious, but such considerations are not always taken into account. If you incorporate drawers into a built-in unit, again make them plentiful and shallow, and consider fronting them with plastic or glass, or use a cut-out section for easy recognition. Also remember

to allow room for garments that are not used every day, such as sports equipment and skiing clothes.

Shoes can be stored on racks; on sloping, pull-out shelves; in clear plastic boxes; or in their original boxes with a Polaroid taped to the front detailing the footwear treasures within (the cheap solution for many storage aficionados).

Do not, by the way, be deterred from installing fitted cupboards just because a bedroom is small. Following the principle of using large-scale furniture in small rooms, a wall of fitted storage can make a small room look larger and, properly planned, will reduce the need for other furniture. Also, bear in mind that it is no good storing something that you cannot easily access when you need it. Although it might make sense to put, say, seasonal clothes away in high cupboards when the season changes, it makes very little sense to use those same high cupboards for things you use regularly.

far left Here a ziggurat of open storage, in translucent plastic with an almost conceptual display of clothing, has been staggered along one side of a bedroom. The regularity and order of such a display is visually stimulating, but also requires a highly methodical approach.

middle left The white sliding doors in this modern space hide a built-in hanging area for clothes. The curved structure to the right has another sliding door that reveals the spiral staircase leading to the next floor.

left Storage spaces in children's rooms should be fun and decorative as well as sensible and practical. This storage area shows how such a balance can be achieved through the controlled use of colour, shape, and texture.

High cupboards play an important part in well-planned storage. This is simply a case of using all the space available. I would recommend building storage right up to ceiling height, even if you think you won't need the space. If the upper section above the hanging and shelf space is designed as deep cupboards, I guarantee those cupboards will soon be filled with all those bulky, awkward things that you feel may come in useful one day, from lampshades to old curtains. Although shelves, hanging rails, and drawers are the most conventional forms of storage, there are other solutions, including boxes, baskets, free-standing rails, and even bags. And storage solutions do not necessarily have to be expensive – shelves divided into different sections, for example, can provide a good basic system, as can different heights of hanging rail, perhaps screened from view by a curtain or blind.

There are now many companies and stores that specialize in storage, offering ideas ranging from the small but clever (plastic pockets for shoes that hang from a hook) to the large and expensive (complete systems tailor-made to fit your room). But remember always to plan the storage around the objects that need storing, rather than the other way round.

Storage space can extend beyond the confines of a single dedicated unit, so do not forget the space beneath the bed that can be used, either informally with shallow containers, or more formally with a purpose-built unit. Awkward spaces can also be adapted to store objects, as with shelving under the stairs or across an obscure corner of a room. A purpose-built space, or possibly an entire dressing area, could even be annexed from part of an area such as a corridor, a hall, a bathroom, or a spare room.

A dressing room is probably the ultimate luxury, and there are many who adore the novelty and self-indulgence of such an extravagance. But it needn't be as grand as the name implies. A compromise solution, and a more efficient one in terms of space usage, is to make a spare room into a dressing room with a bed in it, possibly built within a storage unit.

left Along with dressing rooms, dressing tables are one of the great luxuries of the bedroom. Not many examples are quite as outrageously flamboyant as this gilded and curved extravaganza that positively oozes self-indulgence.

above This more restrained dressing table has a quietly luxurious quality. Everything is to hand: fixed and movable mirrors, drawers of different sizes, and a comfortable stool of the right height.

essentials

Even the most beautifully designed of bedrooms will not work without solid, practical base elements. This chapter looks at the raw mechanics of the bed, offering guidelines to ensure that beds are the right size and shape, mattresses and pillows are supportive and comfortable, and blankets and duvets are of the right weight and warmth. It also offers ten practical step-by-step sequences for bed treatments – ranging from a traditional four-poster dressing to a coronet with drapes, and from a half-canopy to an upholstered headboard.

choosing a mattress

A good mattress is the single most important element in achieving a good night's sleep. A quality mattress can be expensive, however, so research different types before making a decision. There are no industry standards for firmness, and there are always variations between one manufacturer and another. So take your time in the showroom; if you can, remove your outer garments and footwear and spend at least ten minutes in your normal sleeping position on each mattress.

The most traditional mattress has a spring construction. Available as open coil, continuous, or pocketed spring, the matrix of springs compresses under the body to offer support where required. An increasingly popular alternative is the latex mattress. This hypo-allergenic rubber product is formed into a sponge-like mattress core that supports the contours of the body as it moulds around them. A combination of the two, comprising a pocketed spring interior wrapped in latex, provides the best aspects of both options.

There is also the choice of a soft, medium, or firm bed. You should avoid having too soft a mattress that won't give enough support, but equally don't choose one that is so firm that your body makes no impression on the surface. Orthopaedic mattresses can offer excellent support, their robust construction making them especially suitable for a heavier person. If bed partners have incompatible requirements, a mattress comprising two differing halves zipped together can solve the problem.

The performance of a mattress is determined by the bed base on which it lies, and ideally both should be purchased together. The effect of a firm latex mattress on a spring divan base, for instance, will be quite different from the effect of the same mattress on a slatted bedstead. When choosing a mattress for an existing base, try to make sure that the showroom bed base you try it on is of the same type. Also, take into account the fact that manufacturer's sizes are not always standard. Generally, the heavier the mattress, the better its quality and the higher the price. A mattress is an investment, and a good one can be expected to provide optimum support for up to ten years.

A mattress will absorb a surprising amount of moisture over a night's use, and requires regular airing. Turning a mattress from topside to underside and from head to foot not only aids airing but prevents repeated over-use in the same areas. Latex excluded, mattresses attract dust mites and it is good practice to vacuum the surface when changing the bedlinen. Mattress covers create an extra layer of warmth and comfort, offer waterproof protection, and guard against staining, while a hypo-allergenic cover will protect a mattress from dust mites and the allergens they produce.

choosing duvets and pillows

Understanding the properties of different fillings and matching them to your needs is the key to choosing the correct duvet. Natural feather fillings are light, soft, warm, and comfortable with a resilience that results in a longer lifespan. Within this category, duck feather offers the best value for money, duck down adds extra softness, and the luxurious goose down provides more warmth with less weight. Combinations of natural fillings create a duvet with all-round benefits. The first listed ingredient is the dominant one, so expect a duck-feather-and-down duvet to be at least 80 percent feathers, while the stuffing in a duck-down-and-feather duvet will consist of a minimum of 51 percent down. Synthetic fillings are a good alternative to natural ones, especially if you are allergic to feathers or need to wash your duvet frequently. A good-quality synthetic duvet can compare admirably with the warmth and softness of down.

All duvets have a warmth rating measured either in togs or as fill power. The higher the tog or the fill power, the warmer the duvet. To provide suitable warmth for all seasons, duvets can be bought in combination form as two separate duvets. A lightweight duvet for the summer and middleweight one for autumn and spring could then be combined to provide extra warmth for the winter.

Choose a duvet size to match your bed: a king-size duvet on a king-size bed will allow enough width to drape comfortably over the sides of the mattress. If you prefer a billowing duvet style, or have a tendency to battle with your partner for the bedding, then select a duvet one size larger than the bed.

previous pages Any bed, no matter how simple, can be transformed into a bed to remember. Part of achieving this is to ensure that the basic components – the mattress, sheets, pillows, and blankets – are all of the best quality that you can afford.

right This white bedroom is crisp and comforting, with the swathes of gathered fabric suspended from the pelmeted canopy lending prominence to the bed without distracting from the white theme.

left All the patterns in this room are based on geometric and grid shapes, although combined in a free-form, imaginative style. The blue-and-white colour theme ties the various fabric designs together to form a convincing decorative scheme.

When it comes to buying pillows, there is again a choice between natural and synthetic fillings, the emphasis here being on support and comfort rather than weight and warmth. If you prefer to sink your head into a deep, soft pillow, choose down or a traditional feather-and-down mix. In the same way as duvets, there is a variation in the ratio of feather providing the support to down providing the softness. Pure down pillows are the ultimate in comfort, retain their shape well, and are very durable. Good-quality synthetic pillows can match the quality of natural ones, although they tend to bounce rather than sink under your head. Easy to wash and dry at home, they are also far less expensive. Support pillows made from high-density foam can be used on their own, or placed under your usual pillow to provide contour support around the neck and shoulders.

Looking after your duvet and pillows will extend their lifespan. Plump up pillows and shake duvets daily in order for the fillings to air and relax. A duck-feather-and-down duvet can last for ten years, and a goose-down duvet for up to twenty-five years if it is well looked after. Duvets with natural fillings should be professionally cleaned at intervals of five years. It is recommended that pillows be replaced, or at least cleaned, every three years.

choosing bedroom fabrics

If the range of ready-made bedroom furnishings is not to your liking, there are literally hundreds of different furnishing fabrics available – the difficulty is choosing between them. Order swatches of potential choices and spend time combining and comparing them. Note information on width, fibre content, care, pattern repeat, and flame retardant properties on the swatch.

A large pattern can be striking, but when fabric widths need to be joined and patterns matched, a large pattern repeat (sometimes up to one metre or 40 inches) can result in wastage and be uneconomical. Smaller patterns are more versatile, a consideration especially if the fabric is expensive.

Some furnishing fabrics are pre-shrunk and colour-fast, and can be hand- or even machine-washed with care. The majority of manufacturers will advise that fabrics should be dry cleaned, however, although even this process can result in shrinkage. Plan ahead and purchase all the fabric you require at once, as subsequent orders of the same design may come from a different dye batch and show visible variations. All retailers will help calculate the amount of fabric required, and many will offer a making-up service.

If making up furnishings yourself, remember that some fabrics are easier to handle than others. As a rule, natural fibres are better to work with than synthetic ones, cottons and linens being the most user-friendly. Sheer fabrics have a tendency to slip and pucker when sewn and, being delicate, require great care in their handling. Notoriously difficult to work with, velvet demands careful attention when sewn and must be pressed pile-side down on to a velvet board to prevent the pile being crushed. Wools and thick fabrics can be heavy and cumbersome when used in more than one thickness and will require support as they are guided through the sewing machine.

Another good idea is to integrate second-hand or heirloom fabrics into your scheme; the replacement of a lining or the addition of a contrasting border can give such fabrics a new lease of life.

Before cutting, check for any flaws in the fabric. This may involve unravelling large lengths, but it is important as a supplier will not take back a length of fabric that has been cut. Look out for any coloured threads tied to the selvedge, as these usually indicate a flaw.

Before ironing your fabrics, test your iron on an offcut to determine heat tolerance. While some can withstand the hottest steam iron, others will shrink or melt at too high a temperature.

Lining fabrics will protect the main fabric, and if a contrasting colour or pattern is used can add visual interest. Controlling the amount of light entering a bedroom is paramount, and black-out lining will ensure the minimum of light penetration, although its inherent stiffness makes it unsuitable for use with all fabrics. Sewing an interlining between the main fabric and lining will create a heavy, warm, luxurious look, at the same time as protecting delicate fabrics from the effects of the sun.

traditional four-poster bed

A four-poster frame dressed with a back curtain, valance, and ceiling panel creates a grand effect and lends the ultimate in status to a bed within its room setting.

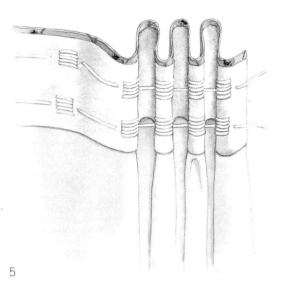

5

1

1 The curtain and valance are hung from **curtain tracks** fixed to the horizontal frame supports. On the exterior of the frame, fix tracks level with the top of the base end and both side supports. On the interior of the frame, fix tracks level with the top of the bedhead end support, plus short lengths along each side.

2 For the back curtain length, measure the drop from the top of the interior back and short-end curtain tracks to the floor, adding a 5cm (2in) allowance at each end. The drop of the valance should measure approximately 35cm (13½in) plus a 7.5cm (3in) allowance. Measure the width of the interior curtain and exterior valance tracks. A generous **pencil-pleat heading tape** requires triple fullness, so multiply the track widths by three and divide by the fabric width to calculate the number of widths needed to make up the curtain and valance.

3 The curtain and valance need to be lined in either a contrasting or a matching fabric. Cut to length the calculated number of widths to length in both the **main and lining fabrics**. With right sides facing, leave 1.5cm (⅝in) seam allowances and machine stitch the main fabric lengths together to make up the full curtain and valance widths. Press the seams open and repeat with the lining widths.

4 With right sides facing, place the curtain and lining together and machine stitch together down the two outer sides, leaving a 1.5cm (⅝in) seam allowance. Press the seams open and turn through to the right side. Repeat with the valance, joining the main fabric and lining at the ends and along the bottom edge.

4

5 Along the top of the curtain, fold over a 5cm (2in) turning on the main fabric and press flat. Repeat along the top edge of the valance, folding the turning towards the lining side. Machine stitch the heading tape along the top edge of both to conceal the raw, turned edges. Draw the cords to gather up the curtain and valance in order to match the track widths. Tie off the cord ends, insert the **hooks**, and hang both on the four-poster frame. Turn the main fabric and lining hem allowances under level with the floor and slip stitch them together by hand to finish the curtain.

6 Measure the top of the frame from side to side and head to foot. Cut out a piece of **lining fabric** to these dimensions, adding a 2cm (¾in) allowance on all sides. If lengths need to be joined to make up the frame width, seam equal amounts either side of a central length. Turn the hem allowance over to the wrong side of the lining around all four edges. With right sides down, align with the top edges of the frame and pin in place.

6

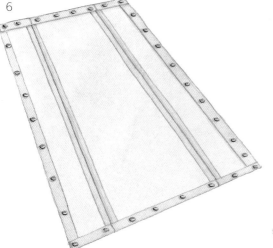

informal four-poster bed

A relaxed, modern style can be achieved using tie-on curtains. When drawn around a simple bed frame, these enclose the bed and form a private sleeping space.

Making eight separate curtains, two to hang on each side, avoids any unsightly seaming in unlined curtains, and allows easier access in and out of the bed when the curtains are drawn.

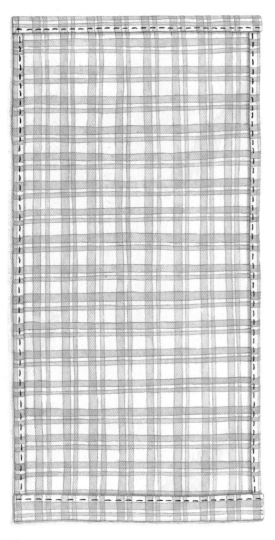

2

1 To calculate how much **curtain fabric** is needed, measure the drop from the bottom of the horizontal support to the floor for the length of each curtain. The full width of all the fabric panels combined should equal one-and-a-half times the perimeter of the four-poster-bed frame. Note that no seam allowances are needed if the edges are to be bound with bias binding, as this envelops the edges without adding or taking away from the fabric dimensions. Trim off any thick selvedges down the sides of each fabric length and zig-zag stitch the raw edges to prevent fraying.

2 If you wish to hem the curtains rather than using bias binding, allow for double 2.5cm (1in) side turnings, a double 7.5cm (3in) hem allowance and a double 5cm (2in) top turning. Starting with the sides, turn in the allowance and press. Pin and machine stitch close to the inner folded edge. Repeat with the turnings at the top and hem.

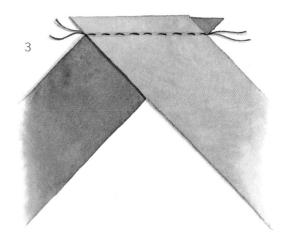

3

3 Ready-made **bias binding** is available in a range of colours to match or contrast with your fabric. To calculate edges to be bound, measure the perimeter of one curtain and multiply by eight. You may find one packet length is not sufficient to bind an entire curtain, and you need to join lengths. To do this, place two strips right sides together at right angles, lining up the raw edges. Machine stitch across the width, leaving a 7.5cm (¼in) seam allowance. Open the seam and press flat.

4 Pin the bias strip on all sides, right-side down, aligning the raw edges. Machine stitch in line with the crease line in the binding. Stop stitching as you near each corner, pinch the binding into a fold, turn, and continue stitching along the next side.

4

5 Fold the binding over to enclose the raw edges and slip stitch down to secure the edges in place, manipulating the corners to form neat mitres.

6 Eight **ties** need to be spaced evenly across the top of each curtain. Short ties will hold the curtain close to the frame, longer ones allowing the curtain to drape on the floor. Cut strips to double the desired tie width, plus 1cm (⅜in) seam allowance. With right sides facing, fold in half along the length and machine stitch down the sides. Turn through with the help of a knitting needle. Neaten the ends and press.

7 Fold ties in half and space evenly along the back of the binding or hemmed turning. Machine stitch to hold in place.

7

corona drapes

Placed above the head of a bed or alternatively along the length of a day bed (as illustrated), this simple fabric canopy combines both elegance and drama.

The canopy is gathered on a **wooden pole** measuring approximately 60cm (2ft), set at right angles to the bed. The pole can be held in **brackets** screwed into the ceiling or secured to a bracket on the wall. **Lightweight fabrics** are best suited to this dressing, since heavy fabrics will not gather on the pole easily.

1 Measure from the top of the pole to the side or end of the bed and down to the floor. Add a 15cm (6in) hem allowance plus a 12cm (4¾in) allowance for the heading. Double this measurement for your final length. One width of fabric should be sufficient to provide double fullness, and a further width can be added to an unlined canopy to create more fullness.

2 Fold the fabric length in half across its width and cut in two. Place the pieces together right sides facing and pin across the width, ensuring any pattern or pile is running in the correct direction. Machine stitch across the width 2cm (¾in) below the top edge.

3 If you are making an unlined canopy, turn the sides under and press a double 2.5cm (1in) hem along the full length of each side. Machine stitch close to the inner folded edge. Repeat with the hems at each end, turning a double 7.5cm (3in) allowance.

4 If using a lining, cut and seam the **fabric lining** (see steps 1 and 2) and turn and stitch a double 7.5cm (3in) hem at each end to match the main canopy fabric. Right sides facing, place the two together, aligning the central seams. Pin and machine stitch along each side leaving up to a 2cm (¾in) seam allowance. Press the seams open and turn the canopy right sides out.

5 With wrong sides facing, fold the unlined or lined canopy in half widthwise along the central seam. Work a line of hand tacking along the top to hold the fold in place.

6

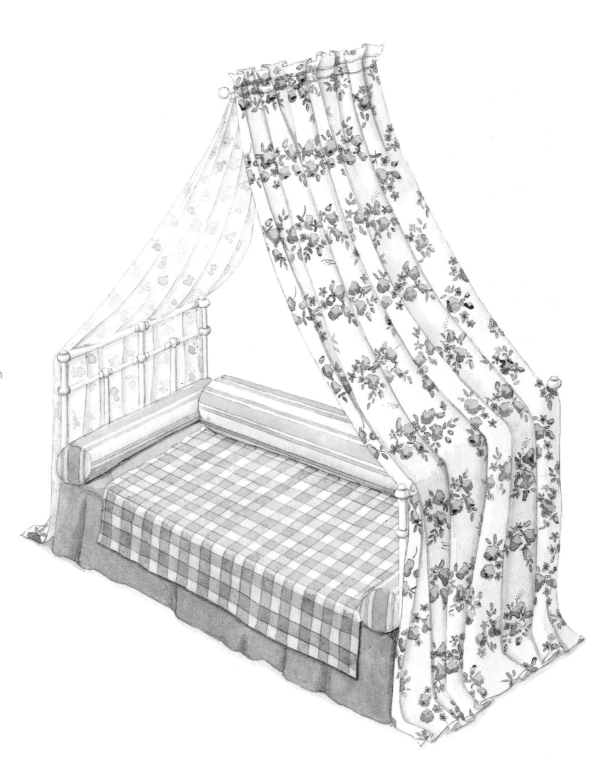

6 Lay the folded canopy flat, and using a **fabric pen**, mark two parallel lines across the width of the fabric. The top line should be set 5cm (2in) down from the top fold, to mark the top of the pole casing. Depending on the diameter of the pole, the second line should be marked between 3cm (1¼in) or 6cm (2½in) down from the top line. Pin each side of the lines and machine stitch along both across the full width of the canopy.

7 Take down the pole and insert it into the casing, distributing the gathers evenly along its length. Hang the pole on the bracket and fix a **finial** on the end to complete the dressing.

coronet with drapes

This dressing will transform the simplest of beds. Without being too elaborate, it can add focus and creates an almost regal air within the bedroom.

These drapes consist of a back curtain and two side curtains: gathered on a semicircular shelf they are then fixed to the wall to form a coronet.

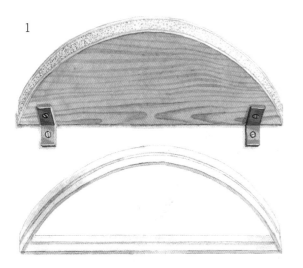

1

1 Draw a semicircle measuring between 40cm (16in) and 50cm (20in) across on a piece of plywood 2.5cm (1in) thick. Cut it out with a small saw, sand the rough edges and staple a length of **Velcro** around the curved edge. Cut lengths of **flexible curtain track** to fit the front curve and the back of the semicircle. Curve the track and fix it to the underside of the plywood. Attach the coronet shelf to the wall using two **angle brackets**, centring it 120–150cm (4–5ft) above the bed.

2 Measure the length of the fabric drapes from the top of the curtain track to the floor. Allow for a double 7.5cm (3in) hem turning plus a 4cm (1½in) top turning. You will need two widths of fabric for the back drape plus one width for each side, the four widths being seamed together to form one large curtain.

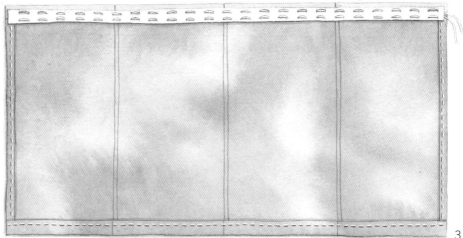

3

3 Cut out the **fabric drapes** and join the widths using a French seam (see sheer dressings on page 158) to enclose all the raw edges. Turn under a double 2cm (¾in) hem down the sides of the curtain, press, and machine stitch close to the inner folded edge. Repeat with the hem allowance. Fold down the top turning and apply a standard **curtain heading tape** along the top, enclosing the raw folded edge.

4 Draw up the strings in the curtain tape to gather the drapes. Tie off the ends to secure, space the gathers evenly, insert **hooks** into the tape, and hang the curtain from the track.

5 Measure the width of the front coronet curve and draw a pattern for the pelmet. The bottom edge can be straight or shaped as desired, with the total drop being no deeper than 30cm (1ft). Cut a piece of **buckram** and a piece of **lining** to the exact size of your pattern. Cut out in the **main fabric**, adding a 2cm (¾in) seam allowance on all sides.

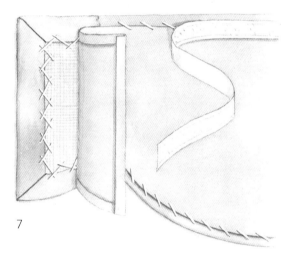

6

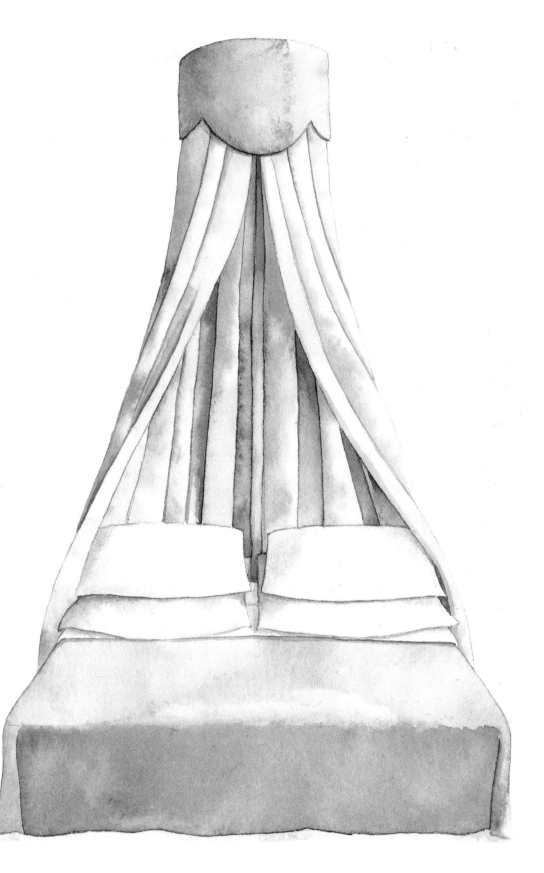

6 Centre the buckram on the wrong side of the main fabric and fold over the allowance on to the back of the buckram, carefully clipping the fabric to ease any tension in tight corners. Secure in place with herringbone stitch or a modest amount of **fabric glue**.

7

7 Fold under and press a 1cm (⅜in) turning around the lining, and place over the back of the pelmet to enclose the raw edges. Slip stitch in place. Glue or stitch the corresponding length of Velcro along the top edge of the pelmet. Hang this on the coronet shelf to conceal the curtain heading and complete the dressing.

half-canopy

The informal awning structure of this canopy is a contemporary statement that accentuates the position of the bed as the focal point within a room.

1 The canopy is constructed from one continuous length of lined fabric. Measure from the floor up to the height at which the canopy will be attached to the wall (approximately 2m 20cm/7ft). Add the length of the bed plus an additional 50cm (20in) to this measurement and cut out the **fabric**. The width of the canopy will ideally match that of the bed – a furnishing fabric width is more or less equal to the width of a double bed, therefore avoiding the need to join widths. Cut out the **lining** to the same dimensions.

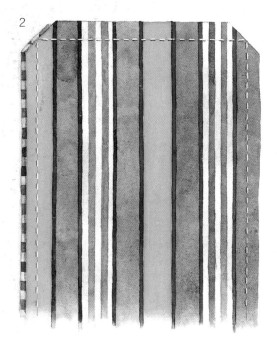

2 Lay the two lengths together with right sides facing and pin down the long sides and one end. Machine stitch along all three edges leaving a 1.5cm (⅝in) seam allowance. Clip fabric at corners.

3 Press open the seams and turn the canopy right side out, pressing again to form flat, seamed edges.

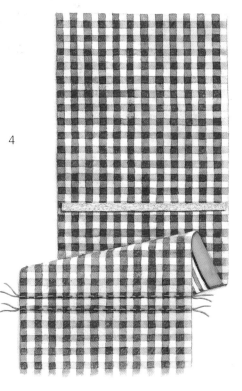

4 Lay the canopy out, lining side up, on a flat surface. Working from the seamed end, mark a line to equal the measurement from the floor up to the height at which the canopy will be attached to the wall. Machine stitch a length of looped **Velcro** across the full width of the canopy at this point. Approximately 1.5m (5ft) down from this, mark two lines set 5cm (2in) apart across the width. Pin outside the lines and machine stitch along them through both layers to form a batten casing.

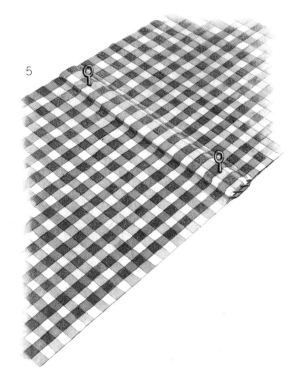

5 Open up one side seam between the two rows of stitching and insert a **wooden batten** at a width of 2.5cm (1in), a depth of 1.5cm (⅝in), and a length of 4cm (1½in) less than the canopy width. Slip stitch the seam to close. Insert two **screw eyes** with an approximate diameter of 1.5cm (⅝in) into the batten, placing them 20cm (8in) from the outside edge.

6 Cut another **wooden batten** to the same dimensions as the first, and screw it to the wall at the calculated canopy height. Staple the corresponding **Velcro** length to the front face of the batten.

7 Secure **two hooks** in the ceiling, spaced to match the screw eyes in the cased batten. The distance they are positioned from the wall will depend on how much of a sweep you wish to create in the canopy ceiling.

8

8 Position the Velcro strips together and suspend the canopy above the bed with **lengths of tape or cord** threaded through the screw eye and tied to the ceiling hook. Roll the raw-edged end of the canopy around a **dowelling rod** cut to the width of the fabric. Hold this in place with another **length of cord** passed through the screw eye and looped under the roll where it is pinned into the underside of the cased batten.

sheer dressings

Delicate by definition, sheer fabrics add an element of magical softness to a bed dressing. These lightweight fabrics can draw practical inspiration from colonial-style bed nets, and can be suspended from the ceiling in generous billows, or simply draped over a bed to soften the hard edges of the bed frame.

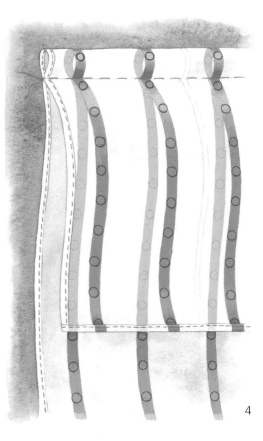

4

1 To make a circular-hoop bed net to suspend from the ceiling above the bed, measure the drop from the point at which the crown will be suspended to the floor. Add 25cm (10in) to this length. Plenty of width can be used, since sheer muslin and voile fabrics gather easily without creating unsightly bulk. An ideally sized hoop of 40cm (16in) diameter will have a circumference of 125cm (4ft). Allow for **four widths of fabric** to provide adequate fullness.

2 Being unlined, widths of sheer fabrics are joined with self-neatening French seams. Place two lengths of fabric together, wrong sides facing, aligning the raw edges. Pin and machine stitch close to the edge leaving no more than a 5mm (¼in) seam allowance. Gently press the seam open, fold the fabric over with right sides facing, and machine stitch a second seam 1cm (⅜in) from the first to enclose the raw edges. Repeat to join the remaining widths.

6 Bunch up the top of the net and wrap a **cord** around its waist to secure it. Loop and tie the other end of the cord to a **ceiling hook** above the bed.

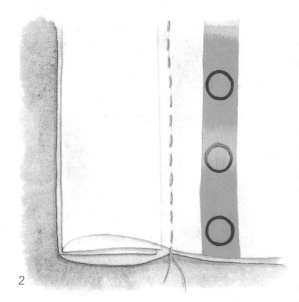

2

3 Turn a double 1cm (⅜in) hem around all sides of the seamed net, and machine stitch close to the inner folded edges.

4 With right sides facing, fold down approximately 60cm (2ft) of the net along its width. Mark and machine stitch a line along the full width 5cm (2in) from the folded edge to form a casing.

5 You now need a **bed net hoop** to support the fabric dressing. Either buy one from a specialist retailer, or make one from the **clear plastic tubing** available from DIY stores. Cut a length to the circumference of the hoop and insert it into the net casing. When all the net is gathered on the tube, join the ends with a **dowelling stopper**.

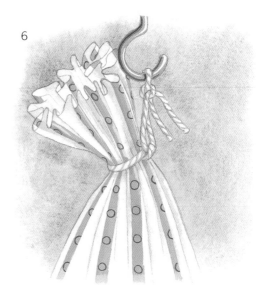

6

An alternative idea for a sheer bed dressing uses a simple framework of poles suspended above the bed, over which the sheer drapes can be arranged.

1 Cut two lengths of 2cm (¾in) thick **dowelling rod** to the length of the bed, plus two to the width of the bed. Mitre the ends, **glue**, and pin them together with tacks to form a flat rectangular frame. Alternatively, cross the rods over at the corners and bind them to secure. Tie **cords** at each corner and suspend from ceiling hooks.

2 Hem a **sheer length of fabric** to the width of the frame, measuring the length of the bed plus 1m (3ft). Simply drape the fabric across the length of the frame, forming a sweep in the centre with tails hanging at either end. Alternatively, position the ties around the sides of a hemmed drape cut to fit the frame, and tie them to the frame.

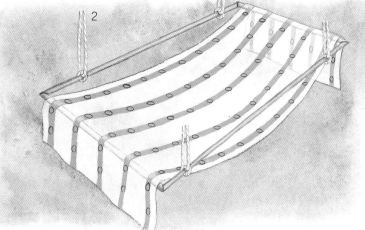

upholstered headboard

The padded upholstery of this headboard offers a comfortable support, and is an attractive alternative to a wooden or metal bedhead. Alternatively, a curtain hung at the head of the bed will offer the same visual focus.

1 The width of a headboard should be the same as the bed width, so measure the distance between the outside edges of the bed frame. The height can be more flexible, but in general the wider the bed, the higher the headboard should be. Some headboards are fixed, with the base sitting on top of the bed frame behind the mattress. Others, such as those on divans, are fixed with the base set level with the top of the mattress. Take this into account when calculating the headboard height.

2 Cut a piece of 18mm (¾in) **plywood** plus a piece of 7.5cm (3in) thick **flame-retardant foam** to the desired size. Aligning all edges, lay the foam on the board, securing it in place with **double-sided tape**.

3 Cut out a piece of **lining fabric**, adding a 15cm (6in) allowance on all sides. Centre the foam side-down on the lining fabric. Pull the lining round to the back of the board and secure with **staples**. Work from the centre of each edge towards the corners, adjusting the tension of the lining as you staple each point on the opposing side. The tension will compress the foam at the edges and create a curved profile. Repeat with the **main fabric**, folding the excess corner seam allowances at the back of the board.

4 Cut a piece of lining to the size of the headboard and fold under a 2cm (¾in) turning. Position on the back of the headboard and slip stitch the edges to conceal any staples.

5 Cut **two battens** to a length of 7.5cm (3in) and a width of 2.5cm (1in). Extend the battens sufficiently below the bottom of the headboard for fixing to the bed base and screw securely to the back of the headboard.

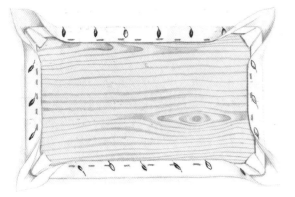

3

5

While not providing the back support of a headboard, a decorative curtain or panel hung against the wall at the head of a bed can offer equal prominence and help to mask an expanse of bare wall.

1 Calculate the number of fabric widths needed to create the desired gather across the full width of the bed. Different styles of ready-made **curtain heading tape** require different amounts of fabric fullness: standard tape should have fabric one-and-a-half to two times its length; pinch pleat tape should have fabric twice its length; goblet pleat tape should have fabric two-and-a-quarter times its length; and pencil pleat tape two-and-a-half to three times its length.

2 Measure the curtain length from the underside of the curtain pole to the floor, adding a double hem and top turning allowances, then cut out the **curtain fabric**. Adding **lining fabric** to the curtain will help it to hang better and will protect it from the effects of sunlight. Since this curtain will hang against a wall, it is not necessary to sew in a lining when making it up.

bed valance

Made in a fabric that can either match or contrast with the bedding, a valance can hide an unattractive bed base and conceal a useful under-bed storage area.

1 Remove the mattress and measure the width of the bed base from side to side, the length from head to foot, and the height from the top of the base to the floor.

2 The central panel of the valance that will be concealed by the mattress is made from **lining fabric** edged with a border of **main fabric**. Cut a piece of lining fabric measuring the width multiplied by the length of the bed base plus a 2cm (¾in) seam allowance on all sides (two lengths of lining may need to be seamed together to make up the width). From the main fabric, cut four strips 15cm (6in) wide, two cut to the length, and two cut to the width of the bed plus a 2cm (¾in) seam allowance at each end.

3 Place the ends of a short and a long strip together with right sides facing. Working from the outside corner, mark a 45 degree angle across the strip end. Machine stitch along this line, trim off the corner, and press the mitred seam open. Continue joining alternate long and short strips together to form a continuous border.

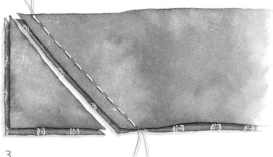

3

4

4 Fold under and press a 2cm (¾in) turning around the inner border edges. Aligning the raw edges, place the mitred border right sides up on the lining fabric and hand tack the two together around all sides. Pin and machine top stitch the turned inner border edge on to the lining fabric to complete the central panel.

5 If using a plain fabric, the long sides of the valance can be cut in one piece along the length of the fabric. If using a patterned fabric, two widths will need to be seamed together to make up the length. Cut two lengths (joining widths as necessary) to the length of the bed and one to the width of the bed, all three measuring double the height of the valance, plus a 2cm (¾in) seam allowance on each side.

6 With right sides facing, fold in half along the full length of each length and machine stitch down each short end, leaving a 2cm (¾in) seam allowance. Clip the corners, press the seams open, and turn the lengths right side out. Press the bottom folds flat to form self-lined valance lengths.

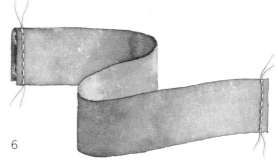

6

7 Using the same technique, make two corner end flaps to a finished width of 30cm (1ft).

8 With right sides together, place the three valance lengths along the corresponding sides of the central panel, aligning the raw edges. Pin in position with the valance ends meeting at each corner. Place the end flaps down to cover the valance ends, clipping the seam allowance to turn the corner. Machine stitch through all layers around the three sides leaving a 2cm (¾in) seam allowance. Turn under and hem the open top end of the valance to complete.

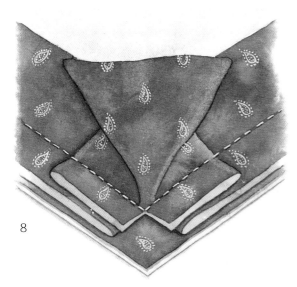

8

duvet cover and pillowcase

A large range of bedlinen is available to buy ready made. However, the advantage of making your own is that it allows you to choose fabrics that match the other parts of your decorative scheme.

Duvet covers and pillowcases should be washed frequently. Choose cotton or linen fabrics that are pre-shrunk and machine washable. It is unlikely that any fabric will be wide enough for a double duvet cover, so seaming will be required. Making a duvet cover to a patchwork design or one with a contrasting border such as the one shown here will solve this problem.

1 Measure the length and width of the duvet, and join pieces of **pattern paper** together to these dimensions. Plan and draw out the patchwork or bordered design on the paper. Then cut along the design lines to make individual pattern pieces.

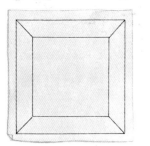

1

2

2 Transfer the pattern pieces to the corresponding **fabrics** and cut them out, adding a 1.5cm (⅝in) seam allowance on all sides. Zig-zag stitch around the edges to prevent fraying. With right sides facing, match the correct pieces and machine stitch them together one by one, leaving a 1.5cm (⅝in) seam allowance. Press the seams open as you work to complete the top side of the duvet cover.

3 The underside of the cover can be constructed in the same way, or it can be made from a plain fabric (two lengths of fabric flat-seamed together will probably be required to make up the cover width). Cut the **underside fabric** to the dimensions of the duvet, adding a 1.5cm (⅝in) seam allowance on all sides. Zig-zag stitch the raw edges.

4 With right sides facing, place the sides together with edges aligning. Pin along the top and sides and stitch around the three sides leaving a 1.5cm (⅝in) seam allowance. Press the seams open and turn through to the right side.

5 Cut a **strip of fabric** 15cm (6in) wide and to a length double the width of the duvet plus a 3cm (1¼in) seam allowance. With right sides facing, join the ends, leaving a 1.5cm (⅝in) seam allowance, and machine stitch them together to form a continuous band. With wrong sides facing, fold the band in half along its length and press flat.

6 With right sides together, slip the band over the open end of the cover and align the edges. Pin and machine stitch through all the layers around the opening. Fold the band over, press, and tuck inside the cover to create a concealed strip on which to secure the **poppers**.

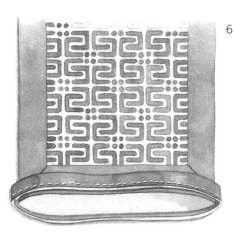

6

7 For a simple, coordinating "housewife" pillowcase, measure the pillow and cut out **front and back fabric pieces**, adding a double-turned 10cm (4in) hem allowance to one end of the front piece, and a 25cm (10in) flap allowance to one end of the back piece. Add a 1.5cm (⅝in) seam allowance around the remaining three sides of each piece.

8 Fold under the double hem on the front piece and machine stitch down close to the inner folded edge. Turn under and machine stitch a small hem along the flap end of the back piece. With right sides facing, place the two together, aligning the bottom raw edges, and machine stitch around three sides, leaving a 1.5cm (⅝in) seam allowance. Fold the flap end over onto the front piece and machine stitch the sides down over the existing seam allowance. Turn the pillowcase through to the right side and press.

8

silk throw and bolster

The modern equivalent of the traditional bedspread, a throw arranged over the bed will add comfort and luxury to cotton bedlinen, while a bolster adds a further stylish touch.

Providing more of a decorative role than a functional one, these items can be made from delicate, textured, and woollen fabrics. While not requiring frequent machine washing, choose fabrics that can be safely hand-washed or dry cleaned.

1 To make this reversible silk throw, cut **two pieces of silk** to the desired length, plus **two equal lengths of interlining**. On a flat surface lay a length of silk right side up on a length of interlining, align the raw edges, and tack the two together around all the sides. Repeat with the second length.

2

2 With right sides facing, place the interlined lengths together and pin around all sides. Leaving a 1.5cm (⅝in) seam allowance machine stitch through all layers around the throw, leaving a 40cm (16in) opening on one side. Turn through to the right side. Turn in the seam allowances at the opening and slip stitch to close.

3

3 Manipulate and pin the seamed edges flat. With a strong matching thread, work a line of hand stitches set 2cm (¾in) in from the edges to enclose the interior seam allowances and form a thick edge.

4

4 Lay out on a flat surface and pin at regular intervals through all layers across the throw. At evenly spaced points, pass a length of strong thread down and back up through all layers, and secure a knot with the thread ends to complete (top illustration). Alternatively, work a pattern of hand-stitched rows across the throw to hold all the layers in place (bottom illustration).

5 Using a **bolster pad** (available in a range of sizes), measure the length of the pad and calculate the circumference (multiply the diameter by 3.142). For a simple cover with extended tied ends, cut a piece of fabric to a width that is the circumference of the pad with a 3cm (1½in) seam allowance and a length that is the length of the pad plus 1m (3ft). Zig-zag stitch the two long sides to prevent them from fraying.

6 With right sides facing, fold the fabric in half along its length and machine stitch the long edges together, leaving a 1.5cm (⅝in) seam allowance to form a tube. Press the seam open.

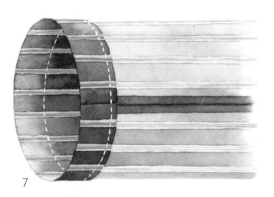

7

7 Fold over a double 2.5cm (1in) turning at each end. Press, pin, and machine stitch around the circumference close to the inner folded edge. Turn through to the right side.

8 Insert the bolster pad, centring it to leave equal amounts of excess length at either end. Bunch up and tie the ends off with **decorative cords and tassels**.

source directory

where to buy beds

Adesso
200 Boylston Street
Boston, MA 02116
Tel: 617 451 2212
www.adesso-boston.com

Alice's of Soho
72 Grand Street
New York, NY 10012
212 966 6867

Baker Furniture
34500 Woodward Avenue
Birmingham, MI 48009
800 59 BAKER
www.bakerfurniture.com

Bloomingdale's
1000 Third Avenue
New York, NY 10022
800 472 0788
www.bloomingdales.com

Bombay
for location nearest you
800 829 7789
www.bombayco.com

British Khaki Furniture
62 Greene Street
New York, NY 10012
212 343 2299

Broyhill Furniture
for location nearest you
877 436 6246
www.broyhillfurn.com

Cabot House
220 Worchester Road
Route 9
Framingham, MA 01701
781 237 2900

Cassina
55 E. 56th Street
New York, NY 10022
800 770 3568
www.cassinausa.com

Charles P. Rogers
55 W. 17th Street
New York, NY 10011
800 582 6229
www.charlesprogers.com

Clive Christian
2930 East 6th Avenue
Denver, CO 80206
303 302 0013
www.clivechristian.com

Crate and Barrel
for location nearest you
800 967 6696
www.crateandbarrel.com

Domain
for location nearest you
877 436 6246
www.domain-home.com

The Door Store
for location nearest you
877 DOOR STORE
www.doorstorefurniture.com

Drexel Heritage
for location nearest you
828 444 3682
www.drexelheritage.com

Ethan Allen
for location nearest you
888 EAHELP1
www.ethanallen.com

Harden Furniture
Hamilton-Wrenn building
200 N. Hamilton
High Point, NC 27262
315 245 1000
www.harden.com

Henredon
800 444 3682
www.henredon.com

Kasala
1505 Western Avenue
Seattle, WA 98101
800 KASALA1
www.kasala.com

Maine Cottage Furniture
Lower Falls Landing
106 Lafayette Street
Yarmouth, ME 04096
207 846 1430
www.mainecottage.com

Michael Taylor Designs
1500 17th Street
San Francisco, CA 94107
415 558 9940
www.michaeltaylordesigns.com

Modern Living
8775 Beverly Boulevard
Los Angeles, CA 90048
310 657 8775
www.modernliving.com

Pottery Barn
for location nearest you
888 779 5176
www.potterybarn.com

Restoration Hardware
for location nearest you
800 762 1005
www.restorationhardware.com

Room & Board
4600 Olson Memorial Highway
Minneapolis, MN 55422
800 486 6554
www.roomandboard.com

mattresses

1-800-Mattress
800 MATTRESS (800 628 8737)
www.mattress.com

Advanced Comfort
800 923 3795
www.abed.com

Bedding Experts
3101 N. Central Avenue
Chicago, IL 60634
888 EXPERTS
www.beddingexperts.com

City Mattress
for location nearest you
716 681 8080
www.citymattress.com

Original Mattress Factory
2349 Cherry Road
Suite 5
Rock Hill, SC 29732
803 327 6444
www.originalmattress.com

Sleepy's
for location nearest you
800 SLEEPS
www.sleeps.com

bed linens

Anichini
800 553 5309
www.anichini.com

Bed Bath & Beyond
for location nearest you
800 462 3966
www.bedbathandbeyond.com

The Company Store
800 323 8000
www.thecompanystore.com

Down Inc.
800 552 9231
www.buychoice.com

E. Braun & Co.
717 Madison Avenue
New York, NY 10021
212 838 0650

Eddie Bauer Home
800 789 1386
www.eddiebauerhome.com

Frette
799 Madison Avenue
New York, NY 10021
212 988 5221
www.frette.it

Garnet Hill
231 Main Street
Franconia, NH 03580
800 622 6216
www.garnethill.com

Indigo Seas
123 North Robertson Boulevard
Los Angeles, CA 90048
310 550 8758

Laura Ashley
87 Main Street
South Hampton, NY 11968
800 463 8075
www.laura-ashleyusa.com

Leron
750 Madison Avenue
New York, NY 10021
800 954 6369
www.leron.com

Linen Closet
1653 McFarland Boulevard North
Suite G4-BA
Tuscaloosa, AL 35406
800 561 7331
www.thelinenclosetonline.com

The Linen Ladies
98 Milwaukee Avenue
Bethel, CT 06801
203 798 8596

Linen Source
800 434 9812
www.linensource.com

Linens & Things
for location nearest you
866 568 7378
www.lnt.com

Lucullus
610 Chartres Street
New Orleans, LA 70130
504 528 9620

Lynnens
278 Greenwich Avenue
Greenwich, CT 06830
203 629 3659
www.lynnens.com

Neiman Marcus Home
800 944 9888
www.neimanmarcus.com

The Old Quilt Warehouse
701 E. 2nd Street
Wichita, KS
800 562 5694

Peacock Alley
83210 Armstrong Avenue
Dallas, TX 75205
800 652 3818

Porthault
18 E. 69th Street
New York, NY 10021
212 688 1661

Portico
450 Columbus Avenue
New York, NY 10024
212 579 9500

Reverie Linens
Montgomery Village
2321 Magowan Drive
Santa Rosa, CA 95405
800 818 0008
www.reverielinens.com

Rosemary Ward
3015 Locke Lane
Houston, TX 77019
713 528 5155

rugs

ABC Carpet & Home
888 Broadway
New York, NY 10021
212 966 4700
www.abchome.com

Current Carpets Design Studio
6033 Skyline Boulevard
Oakland, CA 94611
800 485 8980
www.currentcarpets.com

Darius Antique Rugs
981 Third Avenue
New York, NY 10022
212 644 6600

David Alan Rugs
1009 West 6th Street
Austin, TX 78703
800 284 3255
www.davidalanrugs.com

David E. Adler
6990 East Main Street
Scottsdale, AZ 85251
480 941 2995
www.davideadler.com

Driscoll Robbins
1002 Western Avenue
Seattle, WA 98104
877 206 3387
www.driscollrobbins.com

Fine Arts Rug
1475 Beacon Street
Brookline, MA 02446
617 731 3733
www.fineartsrug.com

Hokanson
5120 Woodway
Suite 6001
Houston, TX 77056
800 255 5720
www.hokansoncarpet.com

Material Culture
4700 Wissahickon Avenue
Philadelphia, PA 19144
215 849 8030
www.materialculture.com

Pande Cameron
815 Pine Street
Seattle, WA 98101
206 624 6263
www.pande-cameron.com

The Rug Barn
234 Industrial Park Road
Abbeville, SC 29620
www.therugbarn.com

The Rug Studio
11700 W. 91st Street
Overland Park, KS 66214
913 310 0800

Salzburg Creations
385 Gerard Avenue
5th Floor
Bronx, NY 10451
718 993 3890

Sisal Rugs Direct
888 613 1335
www.sisalrugs.com

Stark
212 752 9000
www.starkcarpet.com

window treatments

Anthropologie
800 543 1039
www.anthropologie.com

Artisan Interiors
526 South Maine
Middlebury, IN 46540
800 344 7384
www.artisan-interiors.com

Country Curtains
The Red Lion Inn
Main Street
Stockbridge, MA 01262
800 456 0321
www.countrycurtains.com

Everything for Windows
800 BLINDS1 (800 254 6371)
www.everythingforwindows.com

Great Windows
12011 Guilford Road
Annapolis Junction, MD 20701
800 556 6632
www.greatwindows.com

JC Penney
for location nearest you
800 222 6161
www.jcpenney.com

Mary Fox Linton
distributed by Intair C.P.S. Design Inc.
180 NE 39th Street
Miami, FL 33137
305 573 8956

Rue de France
78 Thames Street
Newport, RI 02840
800 777 0998
www.ruedefrance.com

Smith + Noble
800 248 8888
www.smithandnoble.com

Window Treats
One Design Center Place
Suite #236
Boston, MA 02210
617 439 9492

Windows on the World
1855 Griffi Road
Suite A-123
Dania, FL 33004
954 921 8336

fabric companies

Brunschwig & Fils
300 D Street SW
Washington DC 20024
202 554 1004
www.brunschwig.com

Christopher Hyland
212 688 6121
www.christopherhyland.com

Cowtan & Tout
979 Third Avenue
New York, NY 10021
212 753 4488

Duralee Fabrics
www.duralee.com

Donghia
800 DONGHIA (800 366 4442)
www.donghia.com

Henry Calvin Fabrics
151 Vermont Center, #2
San Francisco, CA 94103
888-732-1996
www.henrycalvin.com

Kravet Fabrics
800 648 KRAV
www.kravet.com

Lee Jofa
201 Central Avenue South
Bethpage, NY 11714
800 453 3563
www.leejofa.com

Osborne & Little
90 Commerce Road
Stamford, CT 06902
203 359 1500
www.osborneandlittle.com

Pierre Deux –
French Country
40 Enterprise Avenue
Secaucus, NJ 07094
888 743 7732
www.pierredeux.com

Pierre Frey
12 East 33rd Street
8th floor
New York, NY 10016
212 213 3099
www.pierrefrey.com

Pindler & Pindler
Marketplace Design Center
2400 Market Street
Suite 220
Philadelphia, PA 19103
www.pindler.com

Randolph & Hein
101 Henry Adams Street
Suite #1
San Francisco, CA 94103
415 864 3550
www.randolphhein.com

Scalamandré
942 Third Avenue
New York, NY 10022
800 932 4361

Schumacher
979 Third Avenue
New York, NY 10022
800 332 3384
www.fschumacher.com

Steven Harsley Textiles
Canyon Creek Design Center
4090 Morena Boulevard
Suite A
San Diego, CA 92117
800 776 6999
www.harsey.com

Waverly
800 423 5881
www.waverly.com

lighting

Artemide
9006 Beverly Boulevard
West Hollywood, CA
800 359 7040
www.artemide.com

Authentic Design
69 The Mill Road
West Rupert, VT 05776
800 844 9416
www.authentic-designs.com

Bellacor.com
877 723 5522
www.bellacor.com

Bruck Lighting Systems
3505 L5 Cadillac Avenue
Costa Mesa, CA 92626
714 424 0500
www.brucklighting.com

Fabby
323 939 1388
www.fabby.com

Georgia Lighting
530 14th Street
Atlanta, GA 30318
866 544 4861
www.georgialighting.com

Gracious Home
1217 Third Avenue
New York, NY 10021
212 517 6300
www.gracioushome.com

Hampstead
888 WE LIGHT
www.hampsteadlighting.com

Hessamerica
PO Box 430
Shelby, NC 28151
704 471 2211
www.hessamerica.com

Home Depot
for location nearest you
770 433 8211
www.homedepot.com

Iron Factory
7030 E. Indian School Road
Scottsdale, AZ 85251
888 664 IRON
www.2ndave.com

The Light Shop
7406 Wornall Road
Kansas City, MO 64114
816 444 1820

Lightiforms
509 Amsterdam
New York, NY 10024
212 875 0407

Lighting Inc.
6628 Gulf Freeway
Houston, TX 77087
888 641 6628
www.lightinginc.com

Louis Poulsen Lighting Inc.
3260 Meridan Parkway
Fort Lauderdale, FL 33331
954 349 2525
www.louispoulsen.com

Lowe's Home Centers
for location nearest you
800 445 6937
www.lowes.com

RC Lurie
1024 South Plumer Avenue
Tucson, AZ 85719
520 792 0509

Rejuvenation
1100 SE Grand Avenue
Portland, OR 97214
888 401 1900
www.rejuvenation.com

Sirmos
30–00 47th Avenue
Long Island City, NY 11101
718 786 5920

Urban Archaeology
143 Franklin Street
New York, NY 10013
212 431 4646
www.urbanarchaeology.com

restoration organizations

The organizations listed below will suggest
a suitable conservator or restorer.

Antique Restorers.com
www.antiquerestorers.com

The American Institute for
Conservation of Historic and
Artistic Works
1717 K Street NW, Suite 200
Washington DC 20006
202 452 9545
www.aic.standford.edu

Association of Restorers
8 Medford Place
New Hartford NY 13413
315 733 1952
www.assoc-restorers.com

Canadian Conservation
Institute
1030 Innes Road
Ottowa ON K1A OM5
Canada
613 998 3721
www.cci-icc.gc.ca

Heritage Preservation
1730 K Street NW Suite 566
Washington DC 20006
202 634 1422
www.heritagepreservation.org

Talas
568 Broadway
New York, NY 10012
212 219 0770
www.talasonline.com

index

Page numbers in *italics* refer to captions.

acknowledgments

Mitchell Beazley would like to thank the following interior designers, architects, and location owners for their help with this book:

Block Architecture
83a Geffrye Street
London E2 8HX
Tel: +44 (0) 20 7729 9194
Fax: +44 (0) 20 7729 9193
mail@blockarchitecture.com
www.blockarchitecture.com

Duggie Fields (artist)
www.duggiefields.com

Garthmyl Hall
Garthmyl
Montgomery
Powys
Wales SY15 6RS
Tel: +44 (0) 1686 640550
Fax: +44 (0) 1686 640609

François Gilles Dominique Lubar
IPL-Interiors
25 Bullen Street
London SW11 3ER
Tel: +44 (0) 20 7978 4224
Fax: +44 (0) 20 7978 4334
ipl.interiors@virgin.net

David Hare Designs
Chateau de Lourdines
Cursay sur Div 86120
France
Tel: +44 (0) 20 7792 2373
Mob: 07957 251 002

Harper Mackay Ltd
33–37 Charterhouse Square
London EC1M 6EA
Tel: +44 (0) 20 7600 5151
Fax: +44 (0) 20 7600 1092
design@harpermackay.com
www.harpermackay.com

The Holding Company
241–245 Kings Road
London SW3 5EL
Tel: +44 (0) 20 7352 1600
Brochure order line:
+44 (0) 20 8445 2888
www.theholdingcompany.co.uk

John Miller and Partners
35 Hawley Crescent
NW1 8NP
Tel: +44 (0) 20 7482 4686
Fax: +44 (0) 20 7267 9904
j.miller@johnmillerandpartners.co.uk
www.johnmillerandpartners.co.uk

Julian Muggridge
Brownrigg Interiors
10a Mews Street
Petworth
West Sussex
Tel: +44 (0) 1798 344 321
info@brownrigg-interiors.com
brownrigg-interiors.com

The Old Station Hotel
Coultershaw
Petworth
West Sussex GU28 0JF
Tel/fax: +44 (0) 1798 342346
mlr@old-station.co.uk

Parma Lilac
Visiting by appointment
Tel: +44 (0) 20 8960 9239
Fax: +44 (0) 20 7912 0993
info@parmalilac.co.uk
www.parmalilac.co.uk

Graham Phillips (architect)
www.skywood.com

Vivienne Roberts (interior designer)
1 Cornwall Gardens
London SW7 48J
Tel: +44 (0) 20 7581 8676
vivienneroberts1@aol.com

The Seafood Restaurant/ St Edmunds House
Riverside
Padstow
Cornwall PL28 8BY
Tel: +44 (0) 1841 532 700
Fax: +44 (0) 1841 532 942
reservations@rickstein.com
www.rickstein.com

Ken Shuttleworth (architect)
www.kenshuttleworth.com

St Martins Lane Hotel
45 St Martins Lane
London WC2N 4XH
Tel: +44 (0) 20 7300 5500
Fax: +44 (0) 20 7300 5501
Reservations: +44 (0) 20 7300 5555 (can be connected through main number)
www.ianschragerhotels.com

Todhunter Earle Interiors
Chelsea Reach
1st Floor 79–89 Lots Road
London SW10 0RN
Tel: +44 (0) 20 7349 9999
Fax: +44 (0) 20 7349 0410
www.todhunterearle.com

Also Katherine Clark (milliner) and Mark Denton.

Picture credits

Key: l left, r right, t top, b bottom; OPG Octopus Publishing Group; SH Sebastian Hedgecoe

Front cover: OPG/SH, location The Seafood Restaurant/St Edmunds House; **back cover: centre** OPG/SH, interior designer Julian Muggridge; **top** Andreas Von Einsiedel, **bottom** OPG/SH, architectect Ken Shuttleworth.

1 OPG/SH; **2** OPG/SH interior design Julian Muggridge; **4-5** OPG/SH; furniture by Parma Lilac; **6-7** OPG/SH, interior design IPL Interiors, Francois Gilles and Dominique Lubar; **8-9** OPG/SH, location Old Station Hotel; **10** Andreas Von Einsiedel; **11** Bridgeman Art Library/Galleria dell' Accademia, Venice; **12** National Trust Photographic Library/Bill Batten; **13** Bridgeman Art Library/Rafael Valls Gallery, London; **14** National Trust Photographic Library/Andreas von Einsiedel; **15** Bridgeman Art Library/Private Collection; **16** tl The Interior Archive/Fritz von der Schulenburg; **17** Bridgeman Art Library/Rijksmuseum Vincent Van Gogh, Amsterdam; **18** Bridgeman Art Library/Ferens Art Gallery, Hull City Museums and Art Galleries; **19** National Trust Photographic Library/Mike Caldwell; **20-21** OPG/SH, architects Block Architecture; **22** Narratives/Jan Baldwin; **23** OPG/James Merrell; **24, 25** IPC/Country Homes & Interiors/Trevor Richards; **26** The Interior Archive/Simon Upton; **27** tl Narratives/Jan Baldwin; **27** tr The Interior Archive/Simon Upton; **28-29** OPG/SH, interior design Vivienne Roberts; **30** bl & br Verne; **31** OPG/SH, interior design Julian Muggridge; **32, 33**r & bl Ray Main/Mainstream; **33** tr Verne; **34, 35** OPG/SH, architects John Miller and Associates; **36** tl Ray Main/Mainstream; **36** tr Red Cover/Brian Harrison; **37** The Interior Archive/Fritz von der Schulenburg; **38** Andreas Von Einsiedel; **39** t Verne; **39** b Red Cover/Steve Dalton; **40, 41, 42-3** OPG/SH, architect Ken Shuttleworth; **44** t Ray Main/Mainstream; **44** b Verne; **45** Red Cover/Winfried Heinze; **46, 47** OPG/SH, architect Graham Phillips; **48** t & b, **49** OPG/SH, location Old Station Hotel; **50-51** OPG/Deidi von Schaewen; **52** OPG/SH, interior designer David Hare; **53** OPG/Tim Clinch; **54** The Interior Archive//Fritz von der Schulenburg; **55** OPG/James Merrell; **56** Red Cover/David George; **57** Ray Main/Mainstream; **58** tl OPG/James Merrell; **58** tr & b Red Cover/Andreas von einsiedel; **59** OPG/SH, location Katherine Clarke, milliner; **60-61, 62, 63**t & b OPG/James Merrell; **64** t IPC/Country Homes and Interiors/Spike Powell; **64** b, **65** OPG/SH, interior design Julian Muggridge; **66** The Interior Archive/Fritz von der Schulenburg; **67** tl OPG/SH, location Old Station Hotel; **67** tr OPG/James Merrell; **68, 69** OPG/SH, location The Seafood Restaurant/St Edmunds House; **70** The Interior Archive/Simon Upton; **71, 72** OPG/James Merrell; **73** Andreas Von Einsiedel; **74** The Interior Archive; **75** t Red Cover/Polly Farquharson; **75** b The Interior Archive/Fritz von der Schulenburg; **76** t OPG/James Merrell; **76** b OPG/SH, interior design IPL Interiors, Francois Gilles, Dominique Lubar; **77, 78-9** OPG/James Merrell; **80** bl Andreas Von Einsiedel; **80** br International Interiors/Paul Ryan; **81** Verne; **82** tl & tr OPG/SH, architects Harper Mackay; **82** b OPG/James Merrell, designer Issey Miyake; **83** OPG/SH, furniture by Parma Lilac; **84** Ray Main/Mainstream, architect Simon Condor; **85** Ray Main/Mainstream, designers Collett-Zarzycki; **86-87** OPG/SH, interior design Todhunter Earle Design; **88** tl OPG/SH, location St Martin's Lane Hotel; **88** b Andreas Von Einsiedel; **89, 90** OPG/SH, location Duggie Fields, artist; **91** tl & tr OPG/SH, location Mark Denton; **92-93** The Interior Archive/Andrew Wood; **94, 95** The Interior Archive/Fritz von der Schulenburg; **96** l Ray Main/Mainstream; **96** r The Interior Archive/Fritz von der Schulenburg; **97** The Interior Archive/Simon Upton; **98** OPG/SH, architects Block Architecture; **99** The Interior Archive/Frizt von der Schulenburg; **100-101** Deidi Von Schaewen; **102** l OPG/SH, interior design IPL Interiors, Francois Gilles, Dominique Lubar; **102** r OPG/SH, interior design Vivienne Roberts; **103** International Interiors/Paul Ryan; **104** Deidi Von Schaewen; **105** tl Ray Main/Mainstream, architect Peter Wadley; **105** tr IPC/Living Etc/Debi Treloar; **105** b Ray Main/Mainstream; **106** Andreas Von Einsiedel; **107** Red Cover/David George; **108** Deidi Von Schaewen; **109** The Interior Archive/Simon Upton; **110** OPG/SH, location Garthmyl Hall; **111** tl Andreas Von Einsiedel; **111** tr Red Cover/Robin Matthews; **111** b The Interior Archive/Fritz von der Schulenburg; **112** OPG/James Merrell; **113** Andreas Von Einsiedel; **114** OPG/SH, interior Design Julian Muggridge; **115** tl OPG/Michael Banks; **115** tr OPG/SH, interior design David Hare; **116** bl & br OPG/Michael Banks; **117** OPG/SH, location St Martin's Lane Hotel; **118** tl Red Cover/Jake Fitzjones; **118** tr Arcaid/Gary Hamill Photography; **118** br Ray Main/Mainstream; **119** The Interior Archive/Fritz von der Schulenburg; **120** Ray Main/Mainstream/the Rookery; **121, 122-3** Deidi Von Schaewen; **124-125** OPG/SH, location St Martin's Lane Hotel; **126** OPG/James Merrell; **127** Narratives/Jan Baldwin; **128** tl Ray Main/Mainstream; **128** br OPG/SH, location Mark Denton; **129** Arcaid/Richard Glover; **130** tl and tr OPG/SH, interior design Todhunter Earle Interiors; **131** Ray Main/Mainstream; **132-133** Deidi Von Schaewen; **134** bl Brookes Stacey Randall; **134** br The Interior Archive/Fritz von der Schulenburg, design Richard Mudditt; **135** Red Cover/Andreas von Einsiedel; **136, 137** b OPG/SH, interior design Todhunter Earle Interiors; **137** tr Arcaid/Richard Glover; **138** tl The Holding Company; **138** tr OPG/SH, architect John Miller and Partners; **139** Arcaid/Alberto Piovano; **140** OPG /Deidi Von Schaewen; **141** Narratives/Jan Baldwin; **142-143, 145, 146** OPG/James Merrell; **148-167** illustrations Carolyn Jenkins; **169** OPG/SH, architects Block Architecture; **170** OPG/SH, interior design Vivienne Roberts.